The Real Camelot

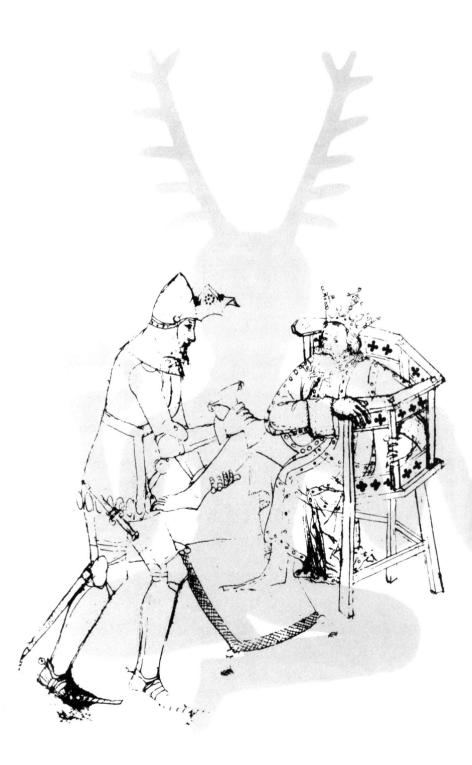

JOHN DARRAH

The Real Camelot
Paganism and the Arthurian Romances

DORSET PRESS

AAA-9113

Library of Congress Catalog Card Number 80-52094

This edition published by Dorset Press,
a division of Marboro Books Corp.,
by arrangement with Thames and Hudson, Inc.

ISBN 0-88029-027-7
(Formerly ISBN 0-500-01250-4)

Printed in the United States of America

Contents

Foreword   7

Introduction   12

PART I
Sacred Kings in the
Arthurian Romances

1 The Challenge   24
2 Annual Kings   37
3 The Dolorous Stroke   53

PART II
The Historical Background of
the 'Arthurian' Sacred Kings

4 Pagan Deities in the Romances   72
5 Time-scale   82
6 Camelot and Sarras   89

PART III
The Pagan Framework underlying
the Arthurian Legend

7 The Birth of Arthur   104
8 The Sword in the Stone   115
9 The Round Table   124
10 Merlin   133
11 Arthur   137

Appendices   141

Notes on the text   149

Bibliography   151

Index   155

Foreword

Books on the historical basis of the Arthurian legends usually concentrate on Arthur himself and pay no attention to the trappings of romance, such as 'the sword drawn from the stone' and 'the Dolorous Stroke'. *The Real Camelot* does the opposite. It has nothing to say of the historical Arthur or the humdrum bric-à-brac disinterred from post-Roman sites, but observes instead the rich pageant of the Arthurian court as a whole. The reality which underlies many well-known inhabitants of Camelot (and, indeed, that city itself) is not to be found in the meagre chronicles of the Dark Ages but in an oral tradition which has remembered the actions of cult figures from the heyday of the native paganism – a paganism already in decline by the time of the Roman occupation.

The wide range of the enquiry involves a large number of separate disciplines. The written material which comes under review is the field of study of more than one literary school, and is also of interest to folklorists and anthropologists; the physical background is in various ways the preserve of prehistorians, archaeologists and Celticists; and the matter is complicated by the fact that the traditional tales used here as sources are preserved in languages different from the original. The works of specialists in all these fields provide the material, whether opinion or fact, from which this book is built. I am heavily indebted to them. I am also aware that, for reasons which will shortly be mentioned, some of the authors quoted might not draw the same conclusions as I have done. The reader should therefore be more than usually on guard to avoid the unwarranted assumption that a quotation implies its author's approval of any inference which might be drawn from it.

The main pillars of my argument have long been recognized. They are the presence in the Arthurian cycle of episodes which recall the priesthood of Diana at Nemi (so vividly described by Frazer); of episodes only to be explained as recollections of annual kingship; and of episodes which recall the significance of virility in the priestly kings of pagan

7

societies. What is, I believe, new is a serious attempt to follow the ramifications of these themes in the French versions of traditional tales which underlie Malory's Camelot; a demonstration of the relationship of the themes to known deities; and a demonstration of their association with artefacts contributive to native cults.

This brief résumé shows that I have ventured into a field adjacent to that of several well-established disciplines, but it is a field into which specialist authors from these self-contained disciplines are seldom tempted to move. There are, I believe, two main reasons for this. First, the French versions of what were originally Celtic oral tales appear to have fixed the material in written form too long after any possible originating circumstance for them to be taken seriously as possible carriers of information about the past. But this appearance of lateness is discounted by the clear references to pagan cult patterns which will be shown to be widespread in Arthurian tales. Second, the oldest Welsh traditional tales are known to offer few pegs on which to hang mythological explanations. Past failures have resulted in a well-advertised embargo on excursions in this direction. This, however, cannot apply to the basic material of this book which, with its close association between cult patterns and characters completely absent from the Welsh tradition, should clearly be regarded as a different (though partly overlapping) sample of the underlying tradition. The Welsh tales are, regrettably, only a tiny survival from a great archaic oral 'literature', far too small a proportion for them to be considered a representative sample. It would be a mistake to use the paucity of events and characters with recognizably mythological antecedents in, say, the *Mabinogion* to argue against the presence of pagan elements in either the underlying tradition or a different sample of it. Curiously, this argument stands a better chance of success in reverse. Though the French material is, like the Welsh, too small a sample to be thought of as representative of the whole, the presence in it of a *positive* correlation with mythological originals could be used by students of Welsh legend to support arguments in favour of pagan origins in cases where the indications from Welsh sources alone are inconclusive.

Though the difficulties of working among so many overlapping disciplines are discouraging, the rewards of success in terms of adding to our understanding of the past could be considerable. This analysis will not only support those imaginative prehistorians who already speak of deities and ceremonies. It gives a lead towards discussing where and when various cult activities took place; it will extend our recognizable Bronze Age 'literature' to more or less Homeric proportions; and it provides a remarkable instance of continuity of cultural patterns and their stability in tradition.

It is perhaps a slight advantage when working in a multi-disciplinary field not to have one's opinions formed by specialization in any one of them, but there are obvious drawbacks. The comments of critics will therefore be more than usually welcome, in so far as they lead to modifications of the model of the past here presented which will make later versions a better match to those most elusive of observed data, the Arthurian romances.

It will be convenient at this point to comment on the sources to be used. There are three distinct types of source giving information about the Arthurian scene, and each gives an entirely different picture of Arthur and – which is more important for this book, since it is about the background rather than the man – his court.

The earliest written mentions of Arthur appear in the Latin works of Celtic Britons. They refer to Arthur as the leader of the Britons in a series of battles against the Saxons (the historical Arthur).

Next come Welsh traditional tales, recorded in Welsh. These, when they mention Arthur, show him in an entirely different light. His adversaries are hags and witches, and he leads a raid on the 'otherworld'. However, there are familiar figures among his supporters, unlike the Latin sources, which make only a brief mention of Mordred.

Finally there is the 'matter of Britain', the group of medieval French stories based on themes from Celtic oral tradition. Here Arthur assumes the role familiar to us from Malory and Tennyson; and here Camelot, the Round Table, the sword drawn from the stone, the Dolorous Stroke and the Grail Quest first appear. And so does Launcelot, who is absent in Welsh tradition. In *The Real Camelot*, it is to works in this last group that I shall most often turn for information, so it must be presented in rather more detail.

Attention was first widely drawn to King Arthur by the imaginative Geoffrey of Monmouth in the 1130s. Some thirty years later Arthurian themes came into vogue in France with Chrétien de Troyes's *Erec*, followed in turn by *Lancelot*, *Yvain* and *Perceval* – the last being unfinished. These, and roughly contemporary stories about Tristan, were in verse and were self-contained and independent, though with common characters and a common centre at the Arthurian court. Over the next few decades the stock of stories increased rapidly, notably with no fewer than four attempts to continue Chrétien's unfinished *Perceval*, with two prologues to the same work, with the romances of Robert de Boron, and with translations into German and Welsh of Chrétien's work (or else of his immediate sources). By about 1220, a new tendency to turn verse romances into prose evolved, and an attempt was made, in what is now known as the Vulgate cycle, to present a group of prose romances as a consecutive and consistent series. The 'matter of Britain' still continued to expand, though at a slower rate, and translations of its components were made into all the main European languages, including English. But it was not until 1469 that Malory produced his edited translation of various French romances, known from its last part as the *Morte Darthur*, and not until 1485 that this book was printed and so became widely read. The fortunate accident that Malory came late enough for his work to be readily understandable today has meant that Arthurian themes, in the form in which he presented them, have remained an inspiration to English writers though neglected in most of the other countries in which the 'matter of Britain' was once popular.

The relationship of the many stories of the 'matter of Britain' to each other, and to the underlying oral tradition, is too large a topic to be dealt with in a brief note. Readers who wish to pursue the subject further should consult the collaborative history by some thirty specialists in the various fields covered: *Arthurian Literature in the Middle Ages*, edited by R. S. Loomis. Here, all that can be done is to indicate where, in the scheme outlined above, the principal sources used in *The Real Camelot* fall.

Since this book is intended for the general reader, I have regarded availability of a source in English to be of prime importance. So the 'challenge' theme (which is the subject of

Chapter I) is illustrated by a quotation from *The Lady of the Fountain*, originally a Welsh translation of Chrétien's *Yvain* (or from a common source) which is now available in English in the Everyman volume entitled *The Mabinogion*. This might seem a late source; the argument for the survival of the 'challenge' theme, however, does not rest on this sole example but on the group of passages reflecting the theme and its components. A satisfactory case could be made if *The Lady of the Fountain* did not exist, but could not be illustrated by a single romance in English.

All the relevant passages in Welsh and most of those in French are available in English translations. Where they are not, the original is given in the notes. Often, the only English version is Malory's. If so, I have not hesitated to use what again might seem a late source. The main pillars of the argument rest on much earlier material or on passages where Malory accurately reproduces the earlier original. So there is no disadvantage in using Malory here, and these references have the great advantage of availability – even familiarity – as well as the charm of his incomparable style.

The names of people and places are often distorted as a result of repetition and copying. The various manuscripts of a romance may give a dozen or more variations on a particular name. For the sake of uniformity I have used Malory's spelling, as given in the index to the Medici edition. These late forms are unrepresentative of the originals, but as no attempt has been made to find meaning in names peculiar to Malory, there is no reason to look behind the familiar forms.

The many references to *The Vulgate Version of the Arthurian Romances*, edited and partly translated by H. O. Sommer, are indicated by *Sommer*, followed by book and page numbers, in brackets in the text; references to Sir Thomas Malory's *Morte Darthur* by *Malory*, followed by book and chapter numbers; and to the collaborative *Arthurian Literature in the Middle Ages* by *Loomis*, followed by the page number. Other references are numbered and listed at the end of the book.

Introduction

Half a century ago, King Arthur loomed through the mists of time somewhat larger than life and not a little tinged with the supernatural. This is how he had seemed to at least twenty generations of British youth, for the arguments that were to lead to the present view (that he was a real man living around AD 500) had not then prevailed. So Arthur appeared to be largely a creation of the imagination. His name did not appear in school history-books and his main habitation, Camelot, could not be identified. Moreover, his court was frequently the scene of happenings difficult to reconcile to the ordinary world. For example, when Arthur was on the point of defeat in single combat, Merlin 'cast an enchantment to' his opponent King Pellinore 'that he fell to the earth in a great sleep' (Malory I 24); then being without a sword, Arthur rode with Merlin to a lake where, reaching from the surface in the centre, was 'an arm clothed in white samite, that held a fair sword in that hand' (Malory I 25); and with the sword was a scabbard 'worth ten of the swords, for whiles ye have the scabbard upon you, ye shall never lose no blood, be ye never so sore wounded' (Malory I 25). In complete contrast to that other childhood hero, Robin Hood, whose successes were always due to human nerve, eye and sinew, the whole story of Arthur, from the shape-shifting that preceded his begetting to his indeterminate end in the Vale of Avilion, was, or at least appeared then, one of fantasy.

Things have changed today. Though no new evidence has come to light, a closer look at the documents in the case has led to the firmly formulated proposition that Arthur was a real man; that he led the Britons against the Saxons in a series of battles, culminating in Badon in AD 518 (or perhaps 490), and that he fell, with his foe Mordred, at Camlan twenty-one years later. The effect of this new view is not necessarily to translate the whole fantastic paraphernalia of the Arthurian court to whatever site may be thought best to represent Camelot in the late 400s or early 500s. Far from it – the reverse is in fact the case. Foreknowledge, magic scabbards,

shape-shifting, floating stones and so on are an embarrass-
ment to the champions of the real Arthur and therefore to be
discarded. We now have to decide what is real, ordinary and
post-Roman in a set of tales which at one time seemed shot
through with fantasy at every level. Out of the whole of
Malory's *Morte Darthur* and other material referring to
Arthur's actions, only the limited list set out at the beginning
of this paragraph is seriously claimed not to be a figment of
myth or romance. Of the rest, even Camelot falls outside the
real category. Leslie Alcock, who was in charge of the excavations at Cadbury Castle from 1966 to 1970, makes the
following comment: 'The truth is, however, that attempts to
identify Camelot are pointless. The name, and the very
concept of Camelot, are inventions of the French medieval
poets'.[1] And the argument which puts Camelot on the unreal
side of the divide between the realities of post-Roman Britain
and the 'figments of myth and romance' will carry a great
deal else with it besides Camelot.

We do not, however, need to write off these less concrete
matters as irrelevant and uninteresting just because they
cannot be tied down to a particular place and time in the real
world. What has happened is that Arthur, like many another
personage important in oral 'literature', has attracted into
orbit round himself material which does not belong to his
period at all.

The scale and range of traditional tales in non-literate
societies (such as existed in pre- and post-Roman Celtic-
speaking Britain) may not be generally realized, but they
covered most of the roles played by written matter today. The
same tales were repeated generation after generation, and no
doubt played a part in moulding the opinions of society. G. S.
Kirk describes them as an 'important means of argument,
persuasion, consolation and communication'.[2] Communication may be expected to include tribal history, law, princely
genealogy, topography and pagan doctrine. These are the
things for which we must search when we revisit 'Camelot'.
The occurrence of this sort of material in stories of the
Arthurian court has been to a large extent overlooked, but
once these Arthurian 'satellites' are examined closely, our
eyes no longer dimmed by the superior radiance of the star
into whose orbit they have been attracted, they have a great
deal to tell about past actions and attitudes in Britain. These

unnoticed 'planets', saved from oblivion by their chance association with the central luminary, have preserved intact, as if untarnished by the terrestrial atmosphere, some record of an earlier age.

We have been directed, by Alcock's forthright remarks, to the French medieval poets as the sole source of information about Camelot. It seems that, at the civilized courts of great nobles in twelfth-century France, demand for literary entertainment was expanding. One of the themes which found favour was the 'matière de Bretagne' – the 'matter of Britain' – the precursor of the Arthurian cycle as we now know it from Malory and Tennyson. At that time, a generation or two after the Norman conquest, itinerant Breton storytellers, who were of course Celtic-speaking, were equipped to offer to a wider market the traditional tales of Wales and Cornwall as well as those of Brittany. As a result, this group of stories acquired its name – the 'matter of Britain' – its Celtic character, and its content of traditional themes.

It is a common opinion that, by the twelfth century, it is too late to hope to find traditional material of the kind briefly described above. By that date, whatever might have survived from the prime of the native non-literate culture would, it is generally thought, have been so much overlaid by invented stories as to be unrecognizable. As a result of this supposition the traditional material associated with the Arthurian cycle has been disregarded. The opinion has never been put to the test. If enquiry had been made, it could scarcely have escaped notice that the 'matter of Britain' has its roots in the native tradition to a surprising extent, particularly that part of the tradition which has its origin in paganism.

Take, for example, the most characteristic feature of British paganism in the centuries before and during the Roman occupation, the cult of the severed head. The native British (the ancestors of the present 'English' inhabitants of these islands as well as those of pure Celtic descent, for the Germanic invaders are now thought to have mingled with the Britons and not to have replaced them) venerated severed human heads. Heads were, to judge by Continental parallels, displayed in specially constructed niches in temples and even hung up by front doors. The heads of battle victims were especially prized. But our forebears were not merely head-hunters. They had a religious belief of some sort in the spiritual value of severed heads. They also believed in the virtues of numerous cult sites, which might be springs, wells, fords, forest clearings, single trees or groups of trees. As well as these, they had many gods, who might be horned like stags, or like bulls, or like goats; and many goddesses, who being often triple in form could vary from representing fecundity and prosperity to war and death. But the head cult was predominant and pervaded all other aspects of Celtic religion. In conjunction with the cult of sacred waters, severed human heads were deposited in wells and springs. Tangible traces of this ritual act are sometimes to be discovered when an ancient cult well is dug out and a human skull is found among the votive offerings. This practice took place in Roman Britain and was probably a religious force much later. In the sixth century, St David contended with a certain Boia, whose wife is said to have cut a girl's throat, after which a spring burst from the ground; and in the seventh, the council of Toledo denounced those who offered vows to wells (or trees or stones) as they would at altars. By then the connection of wells with severed heads was perhaps no longer worth remarking, but this ancient link was remembered in isolated districts of Britain, as were the pagan attributes of cult wells to promote prosperity, health or good-luck, right up to the eighteenth and nineteenth centuries – probably, indeed, until the oral repetition of traditional tales finally ceased in this century as a result of universal literacy and the advent of radio.

There is in the 'matter of Britain' a description of a human head severed and then thrown into a well, an action which might imply the origin of this episode in Celtic oral tradition. An interesting feature of this incident is that, when we come to examine it in detail, we shall find that the two major participants are both linked with the native god of the severed head cult, Bran. This episode from the 'matter of Britain' has retained enough of the fine structure of the original for us to identify it as coming from a traditional source. It is a genuine sample of a British Celtic folk-tale, even though collected in the twelfth century for the entertainment of a French-speaking audience.

When, in the following chapters, the 'matter of Britain' is searched for other episodes which can be recognized as originating in tradition, we shall be able to identify as native to Britain several other cult activities which could previously only be guessed to have taken place from parallels elsewhere.

It may seem surprising that a tradition not stabilized in written form until the twelfth century should be thought capable of carrying, solely by the spoken word, information about a period some centuries before. Yet 'folk memory' of this sort has been noted in examples as far removed as Greece, the South Seas and the Eskimo Arctic. The most striking instance, however, is much more local. It comes from the very century we have been looking at and from a background closely linked with the 'matter of Britain'. Geoffrey of Monmouth, whose somewhat imaginative *Historia Regum Britanniae* was compiled not later than 1139, included an entirely irrelevant story in the section dealing with post-Roman times. He describes how Aurelius Ambrosius (the brother of Arthur's father, Uther Pendragon), wishing to commemorate a group of Britons who had been treacherously slain by the Saxons, asked Merlin's advice on a suitable memorial. Aurelius Ambrosius was told that if he wished for a long-lasting monument, he should 'send for the Dance of the Giants that is in Killare, a mountain in Ireland.'[3] The Giants' Dance is the stone structure of Stonehenge. Geoffrey of Monmouth does not use the name Stonehenge – which first appears in the *Historia Anglorum* of Henry of Huntingdon, written only a few years before Geoffrey's *Historia* – but the siting of the stones of the Giants' Dance near Amesbury leaves little doubt as to the commonly accepted explanation, that Stonehenge is intended. This Merlin proceeded to fetch, and to set up in its present position. It is, of course, now known that Geoffrey was wrong. The first stones of Stonehenge were almost certainly erected some 2,500 years before the period of which Geoffrey was speaking. R. J. C. Atkinson gives 2100–2000 BC for the erection of the bluestone circle.[4] But there is a remarkable correspondence between one factor in Geoffrey's description and the actual construction of Stonehenge. The first stone structure really was brought by sea from the west, not, it is true, Ireland but south-west Wales. This is a fact which could not be deduced from the stones themselves until geology became an established science. A distant origin for the bluestones was never suspected in recent times right up to the nineteenth century, and the actual source of most of these stones in a restricted area of the Prescelly Mountains was not known until 1923. A distant origin and carriage by ship are points of correspondence between tradition and original event which are not likely to have arisen by coincidence nor by a rational attempt to explain the existence of the stone structure. As Professor Stuart Piggott remarks in his discussion of Geoffrey's sources:

Twelfth-century science was hardly sufficiently advanced to question the presence of spotted dolerites in a cretaceous landscape, and while Wiltshiremen would know sarsens for the local rocks they were, the only popular theory to account for their origin by visitors seems to have been, that they were artificially made from a sort of Druidic cement. While the building itself might well be regarded as the work of giants or of wizardry, it would be unnecessary to invoke the transportation of its stones from afar – stones were just stones and might occur anywhere, and only their arrangement in an architectural manner as at Stonehenge would call for comment. In parenthesis I think it not unlikely that the absence of any early medieval records of other stone circles, including Avebury, is due to the fact that they were regarded as natural objects of the countryside, in which by a whim of the creator the stones stood on end and in some sort of order.[5]

Professor Stuart Piggott suggests a possible explanation of the mechanism by which the transference of information over many centuries could have occurred. If we consider a closed society such as a priesthood, it is easy enough to imagine the chanting of hymns which would maintain the actions of the founding fathers fresh in the minds of worshippers. He points out that:

We have archaeological evidence of the continuity of use of a certain type of ritual structure or temple, with presumably an accompanying tradition of priestcraft and sacred legend, from the Early Bronze Age to the Roman Occupation, and what scraps of information we have do not preclude its even later survival into the pagan Dark Ages along with other elements of prehistoric cults. Such a continuity would provide a possible vehicle of transmission of legend from an early period into literate times . . . .

He goes on to say that if we accept the implications contained in the arguments put forward in his paper, then:

We must also accept a literary survival which though meagre and barbaric, would nevertheless be of the same order as that of the Mycenaean elements preserved in Homer. In the story of Stone-

henge in Geoffrey of Monmouth we may have the only fragment left
to us of a native Bronze Age literature – a literature which would be
as natural an outcome of a heroic culture such as the Wessex Bronze
Age (or that of Mycenae, with which indeed it traded), as are the
gold hilted daggers of the warriors, but so infinitely more perishable.
We may have a story of the builder, and of the building of the great
monument to the spiritual and political ascendancy of Bronze Age
Wessex, handed down as part of the sacred lore of its priests long
enough to ensure its incorporation in the legends accumulating
round another Wessex leader, a Roman of the Dark Ages; then
preserved in the myths of the Celtic west and finally entering the
body of written record of the Middle Ages among the legendary
miscellanea of a romantic medieval ecclesiastic who may have
fancied it as a fairy-tale.

   This literary survival shows that information from the
remote past can sometimes be preserved in traditional tales.
We should not be too critical of Geoffrey of Monmouth for
making a mistake about the period to which his source
referred. The oral tradition tends to lack historical perspective, and when we come to examine episodes from the 'matter
of Britain' which we can tell from their content to be of
ancient origin, we shall not find it easy to decide the date of
the originating circumstance. The case of the 'Giants' Dance'
is exceptional in referring to a recognizable, datable event.
However, this case is so close to the field in which we shall be
working that we shall be able to use it as a point of reference,
and to recognize from it more fragments of our Bronze Age
'literature' among the traditions of various origins which we
shall be observing. These newly-recognized associates of the
'Giants' Dance' motif will tell us the names of the deities
involved in that momentous episode in our prehistory.
   It is a great pity that we have to rely for this information on
a tradition which has, in addition to all its other vicissitudes,
been preserved in an alien language. But, as it happens, the
earlier and more direct Welsh equivalent does not produce
the same clear indications of pagan origin. This may be the
accident of survival, or it may reflect, at that earlier period
when all the literate were clerics, a specific block on the
writing down of what could then have been recognized as
pagan themes. Whatever the reason may be, the early Welsh
legends, taken on their own, do not lend themselves to
mythological explanations. It is not that deities are absent

from the pages of, say, *The Mabinogion*; merely that most of the divine attributes of those whose names do appear have been forgotten. Apart from a few exceptions which will be mentioned later, we can no longer see these Welsh deities in the round.

In spite of the absence of revealing detail, the Welsh legends in their oldest form often display an archaic quality which is missing in the 'matter of Britain'. No doubt the courtly audiences the French versions were intended for would have rejected as excessively bucolic such authentic features as the way Gwydion son of Don obtained by deception the first pigs in Wales from Pryderi (who had them from the 'otherworld'), and how Gilfaethwy son of Don slept with Math's 'footholder'. Yet these are the very stuff of myth. The latter episode in particular will serve as an introduction to the most prominent feature in the analysis of native pagan customs which follows in subsequent chapters. Math is described as lord over Gwynedd in north Wales, but he was not a ruler of the same kind as the tough prototypes of the Tudors who were ruling the petty kingdoms of Wales during the Dark Ages. He was, in fact, virtually immobilized by a strange custom. For Math 'might not live save while his two feet were in the fold of a maiden's lap, unless the turmoil of war prevented him'.[6] Here we have an ancient attribute of kingship. From this description, Math can be recognized as a sacred king of the sort described by Freud (quoting from Frazer) in *Totem and Taboo* as living

hedged in by ceremonious etiquette, a network of prohibitions and observances, of which the intention is not to contribute to his dignity, much less to his comfort, but to restrain him from conduct which, by disturbing the harmony of nature, might involve himself, his people, and the universe in one common catastrophe. Far from adding to his comfort, these observances, by trammelling his every act, annihilate his freedom and often render the very life, which it is their object to preserve, a burden and a sorrow to him.[7]

The effect on the sacred king's capacity to rule is as follows:

Kings, crushed by the burden of their holiness, became incapable of exercizing their power over real things and had to leave this to inferior but executive persons who were willing to renounce the honours of royal dignity.[8]

Math clearly suffered a prohibition on placing his feet on the ground, a prohibition on sacred kings not unknown elsewhere. He also, as the following passage shows, had to delegate the running of his kingdom to others. Math

> found his tranquillity at Caer Dathyl in Arfon, and he might not go the circuit of the land, save Gilfaethwy son of Don and Gwydion son of Don, his nephews, his sister's sons, and the war band with them, would go the circuit of the land in his stead . . . and the maiden was with Math at all times . . . .[9]

The close correspondence between the affairs of Math and those of other sacred kings makes it probable that this Welsh legend contains a recollection of the real past, and though there may not be chapter and verse from elsewhere for the virgin 'footholder', there is a good chance that at one time Welsh priestly rulers were attended in some such way. The group of stories in which this account of Math appears probably received its final form after A D 1000. It is unlikely to have been a current practice then, but how long it had been a matter of oral literature at that time it is impossible to say.

The picture of the past which we can build up by studying the native tradition will show that sacred kings whose lives were far more drastically curtailed than Math's were a feature of pre-Christian religion. They acted out life-and-death dramas in the full view of their watching people. Here, again, a phrase may be culled from the Welsh stories which is particularly illuminating. When Pwyll prince of Dyfed (the 'w' in Pwyll has the 'oo' sound of 'w' in 'cwm') became ruler of the 'otherworld' for a year in place of its king, Arawn, he did so on condition that he should fight a battle at a ford at the year's end, on the outcome of which his position as king would depend. That the event was a matter of the widest public concern is made clear: 'On that appointed night, the tryst was as well remembered by the man who dwelt furthest in the whole kingdom'[10] as by Pwyll himself. In almost every instance in which we shall recognize a sacred king by his conspicuous behaviour, he is supported in his lonely role by the populace at large, who rejoice that he should by his self-sacrifice preserve them from the threat of catastrophe, who greet him on his accession with processions, music and song, who shed a compassionate tear at his dreadful fate, and who, when he has been deposed, pelt him with offal and drive him out of the town with taunts and jeers.

The glimpses of the real past which can occasionally be caught in both Welsh and French traditional tales usually originate in a religious act of some sort. 'Heads in wells', the 'footholder' and the 'year-end battle at the ford' are all of this nature. They are not figments of the imagination. They represent the actions of real men and women carried out at particular times, perhaps in sequence over very long periods, and at particular places. The time-scale is extremely difficult to fix, for the recollection of a datable event like the moving of the bluestones is unusual. The sites of cult practices, on the other hand, are frequently named though it will not always be possible to discover the present-day equivalents.

As far as the period in time of the pagan originating circumstances is concerned, we have already extended our range of enquiry far beyond the confines of the few decades on each side of A D 500 during which the historical Arthur may be supposed to have lived, and the sites named in the chronicles are completely irrelevant to the location of the cult sites under discussion. But what of the principal Arthurian situation of the romances, Camelot? It has been discarded by the historians as 'an invention of the French medieval poets', but does it really belong to the underlying tradition and if so, to what age does it belong and where shall we find it? This last question is only new in so far as we are now asking it of a Camelot divorced from its post-Roman connotations. Previous answers, always with the period of the Saxon invasion in mind, have been Winchester, by Malory; somewhere in Wales, by Caxton; and Cadbury Castle, by Leland. None of these is supported by a close examination of the French medieval poets, who are our sole source of information on Camelot. The 'matter of Britain' is singularly uninformative about the locations of the places it mentions. Some of them, of course, have modern names such as Salisbury, London and Winchester. These three (the most frequent of this category that appear in the index of Sommer's *Vulgate Version of the Arthurian Romances*) happen to have pre-English roots and so may well represent the original places in those situations. But for the rest we are left almost completely in doubt. Apart from occasional references to countries and named rivers, there are no clues at all for a whole category of descriptive names such as the Dolorous Tower, the Castle of the Border, the Red City and the Castle of the White Thorn. And we are no better off with town names. None of the places without modern names, which make the background for the most important events of the romances can be pinpointed on a map. Bedingran, Carduel, Trebes, Corbenic (Malory's Carbonek), Vandeberes, Sarras and Camelot all come into this class. The answer of the 'matter of Britain' to the question 'Where?' is always vague. But if, instead, we ask 'What?' the replies will be far more informative. Of Camelot, for example, we are told that it was, at a time considerably before that of the historical Arthur, the richest city of the Sarrasens in this country, where the pagan king was crowned, and the most important seat of paganism.[11] Is this, then, the Camelot which has been rejected by the historians who wrote of the post-Roman Arthur? Is this unexpected description a recollection of some real original and not a piece of imagined nonsense? These questions will be answered in the affirmative in the analysis of the 'matter of Britain' which follows, and the 'Sarrasens' will be distinguished from those other pagans of a similar name, with whom the French poets inevitably confused them. We shall see that not only Camelot but several others of the places with romantic names were in fact cult sites. We shall discover the rituals performed in them, and learn of the native sacred kings and how and why they were killed. We shall even hear distant reverberations of the shouts of the watching populace. And when we have established the framework of interlocking cult-patterns with their associated deities and their human substitutes, which were the originals of a substantial section of the 'matter of Britain', we shall find that most of the rest of the Arthurian story has a greater affinity with this strange scene from the pagan past than it has with the Iron Age remains at Cadbury Castle.

PART I

Sacred Kings
in the
Arthurian Romances

1 The Challenge

The objective of this and the following two chapters is to show that some aspects of the romances can be recognized as having their origin in oral tradition. Episodes will be compared with earlier activities which have left tangible traces or which have been described by literate observers of European native paganism.

There are a number of widely accepted examples of traditions which have preserved information through a period of illiteracy lasting some centuries. The 'Giants' Dance', coming from the same century and the same mixture of Welsh and French cultural backgrounds as the 'matter of Britain', is of particular interest here. Two other instances come from Homer. One is the description of an object, a helmet encrusted with boar's teeth, which had been obsolete for a long period before Homer wrote of it but which exactly corresponds to Bronze Age helmets recovered by archaeologists. The other is a description of an aspect of society, the pattern of power in Mycenaean times: in the 'Catalogue of Ships', Homer details the size of various cities' contingents which have been discovered as a result of excavation to be in proportion to the importance of the cities in Mycenaean times, but which do not at all correspond to the sizes of the same cities in Homer's own time. Since writing had fallen out of use in the intervening period, these recollections must have depended on oral repetition. Homer may seem a far cry from medieval Welsh bards, but the societies in which both lived were cast in the same 'heroic' mould, of Indo-European origin, so the system of verbal repetition of one may well have been matched by the other, both in technique and in effectiveness.

We have, then, precedents for the survival of tradition over long periods in the absence of writing. We have also British examples, which are not restricted to Welsh sources. And we have an indication from the instances so far examined, and particularly from the probable channel of communication of the removal of the bluestones, that in the local circumstances there is a premium on the survival of religious matters. Religion will therefore be a suitable starting point for our enquiries. But first there is a point to be cleared up about the extent to which characters in the Arthurian cycle are to be thought of as tied to the post-Roman period by their association with Arthur. It has already been suggested that (apart from wholly imagined additions) unconnected traditional material will have been attracted into the Arthurian 'orbit'. We may reasonably expect any individual figures involved in this transfer to have become naturalized in their new surroundings and indistinguishable from the native residents of the Arthurian court. Arguments to be made in this and later chapters will identify some of these interlopers by their pagan behaviour, and they will have to be prised out of the niches to which they seem by long association to belong.

To take an example: Are we to think of a less important character such as King Pellinore of the Isles as a real inhabitant of Dark Age Britain? Pellinore took Arthur's horse in one episode, and fought with him in another. But he also pursued a wholly imaginary creature called the Questing Beast; he fathered Sir Tor on the wife of Aries the cowherd; the severed head of his daughter Eleine, by the Lady of the Rule, was found beside a well; his legitimate daughter died through bleeding a dish of blood for the custom of a castle; and he was subjected to a spell by Merlin, which rendered him unconscious. These odd associations suggest that Pellinore's feet are not entirely set in reality. But the part he plays is peripheral to the main Arthurian story. There will be no cause for concern if the weight of numerous other associations later shows that he belongs to the older pagan tradition and not to the fifth/sixth centuries AD. The story will continue uninterrupted in his absence. Far more central characters than Pellinore will be shown to belong to this mythological substratum, and when we come to disentangle these immaterial beings from the real world of post-Roman times, well-established links, which might have been thought essential to the plot, will be severed.

The starting point of this enquiry is, as stated above, religion. A great deal is known about the last phase of British paganism and the salient features, including the inconspicuous sites at which worship took place, have already been mentioned. Our search is to begin among these sites. It might not be thought that a single significant action would have been performed in the romances at such everyday places as springs (often called fountains), fords, forest clearings or solitary trees; but a common factor exists. All are sites of single combat between knights, and there is reason to believe that some such combats may have been a cult activity. Whether a particular episode can be recognized as of pagan origin depends on the presence of certain details in the description of the action which will distinguish it from the casual violence which is so prevalent in the Arthurian Cycle. The identifying features are those which characterize the strange priesthood, still existing in classical times, of the sacred grove of Diana at Nemi in Italy – the priesthood which Frazer wrote *The Golden Bough* to explain. They are:

1 A sacred site,
2 which contains a significant natural feature,
3 is defended by a particular individual with his life.
4 An opponent may by a specific act challenge the defender to fight.
5 The challenger, if successful, takes over the defence of the site,
6 and takes the defendant's title and possessions (including in some cases his wife or daughter)

These features are to be observed in Frazer's description of the events at Nemi and they are frequently to be found in British traditional tales, though not always all six together, as will later be shown.

Frazer's account is as follows.[12]

THE KING OF THE WOOD

Who does not know Turner's picture of the Golden Bough? The scene, suffused with the golden glow of imagination in which the divine mind of Turner steeped and transfigured even the fairest natural landscape, is a dream-like vision of the little woodland lake of Nemi – 'Diana's Mirror,' as it was called by the ancients. No one who has seen that calm water, lapped in a green hollow of the Alban hills, can ever forget it. The two characteristic Italian villages which slumber on its banks, and the equally Italian palace whose terraced gardens descend steeply to the lake, hardly break the stillness and even the solitariness of the scene. Dian herself might still linger by this lonely shore, still haunt these woodlands wild.

In antiquity this sylvan landscape was the scene of a strange and recurring tragedy. On the northern shore of the lake, right under the precipitous cliffs on which the modern village of Nemi is perched, stood the sacred grove and sanctuary of Diana Nemorensis, or Diana of the Wood. The lake and the grove were sometimes known as the lake and grove of Aricia. But the town of Aricia (the modern La Riccia) was situated about three miles off, at the foot of the Alban Mount, and separated by a steep descent from the lake, which lies in a small crater-like hollow on the mountain side. In this sacred grove there grew a certain tree round which at any time of the day, and probably far into the night, a grim figure might be seen to prowl. In his hand he carried a drawn sword, and he kept peering warily about him as if at every instant he expected to be set upon by an enemy. He was a priest and a murderer; and the man for whom he looked was sooner or later to murder him and hold the priesthood in his stead. Such was the rule of the sanctuary. A candidate for the priesthood could only succeed to office by slaying the priest, and having slain him, he retained office till he was himself slain by a stronger or a craftier.

The post which he held by this precarious tenure carried with it the title of king; but surely no crowned head ever lay uneasier, or was visited by more evil dreams, than his. For year in year out, in summer and winter, in fair weather and in foul, he had to keep his lonely watch, and whenever he snatched a troubled slumber it was at the peril of his life. The least relaxation of his vigilance, the smallest abatement of his strength of limb or skill of fence, put him in jeopardy; grey hairs might seal his death-warrant. To gentle and pious pilgrims at the shrine the sight of him might well seem to darken the fair landscape, as when a cloud suddenly blots the sun on a bright day. The dreamy blue of Italian skies, the dappled shade of summer woods, and the sparkle of waves in the sun, can have accorded but ill with that stern and sinister figure. Rather we picture to ourselves the scene as it may have been witnessed by a belated wayfarer on one of those wild autumn nights when the dead leaves are falling thick, and the winds seem to sing the dirge of the dying year. It is a sombre picture, set to melancholy music – the background of forest showing black and jagged against a lowering and stormy sky, the sighing of the wind in the branches, the rustle of the withered leaves under foot, the lapping of the cold water on the shore, and in the foreground, pacing to and fro, now in twilight and now in gloom, a dark figure with a glitter of steel at the shoulder whenever the pale moon, riding clear of the cloud-rack, peers down at him through the matted boughs. . . .

Within the sanctuary at Nemi grew a certain tree of which no branch might be broken. Only a runaway slave was allowed to break off, if he could, one of its boughs. Success in the attempt entitled him to fight the priest in single combat, and if he slew him he reigned in his stead with the title of King of the Wood (*Rex Nemorensis*). . . .

Of the worship of Diana at Nemi some leading features can still be made out. From the votive offerings which have been found on the site, it appears that she was conceived of especially as a huntress, and further as blessing men and women with offspring, and granting expectant mothers an easy delivery. Again, fire seems to have played a foremost part in her ritual. For during her annual festival, held on the thirteenth of August, at the hottest time of the year, her grove shone with a multitude of torches, whose ruddy glare was reflected by the lake; and throughout the length and breadth of Italy the day was kept with holy rites at every domestic hearth. Bronze statuettes found in her precinct represent the goddess herself holding a torch in her raised right hand; and women whose prayers had been heard by her came crowned with wreaths and bearing lighted torches to the sanctuary in fulfilment of their vows.

. . . . Diana did not reign alone in her grove at Nemi. Two lesser divinities shared her forest sanctuary. One was Egeria, the nymph of the clear water which, bubbling from the basaltic rocks, used to fall in graceful cascades into the lake at the place called Le Mole, because here were established the mills of the modern village of Nemi. . . .

Women with child used to sacrifice to Egeria, because she was believed, like Diana, to be able to grant them an easy delivery.

The other of the minor deities at Nemi was Virbius. Legend had it that Virbius was the young Greek hero Hippolytus, chaste and fair, who learned the art of venery from the centaur Chiron, and spent all his days in the greenwood chasing wild beasts with the virgin huntress Artemis (the Greek counterpart of Diana) for his only comrade. . . .

When Virbius offended the sea-god, Diana hid her favourite in a thick cloud, disguised his features by adding years to his life, and then bore him far away to the dells of Nemi, where she entrusted him to the nymph Egeria, to live there, unknown and solitary, under the name of Virbius, in the depth of the Italian forest. There he reigned a king, and there he dedicated a precinct to Diana.

The most easily accessible British story which contains the six listed identifying features is the Welsh *The Lady of the Fountain*. This is not a particularly early version as it shows Norman-French influence, and it is difficult to determine to what extent it owes its plot to Chrétien de Troyes's *Yvain*. But the question of who wrote it need not detain us here. A fly preserved is a mark of amber, whoever shaped the jewel.

The part of *The Lady of the Fountain* which contains the sequence of events which may be briefly referred to as 'the challenge' is preceded by two episodes which are not without interest themselves. The first concerns a black giant with one eye and one leg who behaves as lord of the animals. This unlikely creature embodies in his colour and physical peculiarities several elements of pagan thinking. The second, a rainmaking charm, is clearly pagan. Their presence strengthens the argument that 'the challenge' which follows has its origin in paganism. Our piece of amber has preserved three relics of the past, not one.

The relevant part of *The Lady of the Fountain* runs as follows.[13]

The route to the fountain and the adventures to be met on the way are described to an earlier visitor in the following words:

rise early and take the road thou camest through the valley until thou enter the forest thou camest through, and some distance into the forest a byway will meet thee on thy right, and journey along that until thou come to a great clearing as of a level field, and a mound in the middle of the clearing, and a big black man shalt thou see on the middle of the mound who is not smaller than two of the men of this world. And one foot has he, and one eye in his forehead's core; and he has a club of iron, and thou canst be sure that there are no two men who would not find their full load in the club. But his is not an ugly disposition; yet he is an ugly man, and he is keeper of that forest. And thou shalt see a thousand wild animals grazing about him. And ask him the way to go from the clearing, and he will be gruff with thee, but even so he will show thee a way whereby thou mayest have that thou art seeking. . . .

The visitor, Cynon, followed these instructions and reported:

I greeted the black man, but he spoke nothing to me save incivility. And I asked him what power he had over the animals. 'I will show thee, little man,' said he. And he took the club in his hand, and with it struck a stag a mighty blow till it gave out a mighty belling, and in answer to its belling wild animals came till they were as numerous as the stars in the firmament, so that there was scant room for me to stand in the clearing with them and all those serpents and lions and vipers and all kinds of animals. And he looked on them and bade them go graze. And then they bowed down their heads and did him obeisance, even as humble subjects would do to their lord.

And he said to me, 'Dost see then, little man, the power I have over these animals?' And then I asked the way of him, and he was rough with me, but even so he asked me where I wanted to go, and I told him what kind of a man I was and what I was seeking, and he then showed me. 'Take,' said he, 'the path to the head of the clearing, and climb the slope up yonder till thou come to its summit. And from there thou shalt see a vale like a great waterway; and in the middle of the vale thou shalt see a great tree with the tips of its branches greener than the greenest fir trees. And under that tree is a fountain, and beside the fountain is a marble slab, and on the slab there is a silver bowl fastened to a silver chain, so that they cannot be separated. And take up the bowl and throw a bowlful of water over the slab, and then thou wilt hear a great peal of thunder; and thou will fancy that heaven and earth are quaking with the peal. And after the peal there shall come a cold shower, and it will be hard for thee to bear that and live. And hailstones will it be, and after the shower there will be clear weather, but there shall not be one leaf on the tree that the shower will not have carried away. And thereupon a flight of birds shall come to alight on the tree, and never hast thou heard in thine own country a song so delightful as that they shall sing. And even when thou shalt be most enraptured with the song, thou shalt hear a great panting and groaning coming towards thee along the valley. And thereupon thou shalt see a knight on a pure black horse, and a garment of pure black brocaded silk about him, and a pennon of pure black bliant upon his spear. And he will fall on thee as briskly as he can. If thou flee before him, he will overtake thee; if, on the other hand, thou abide his coming, and thou on a horse, he will leave thee on foot. And if thou find not trouble there, thou needst not look for trouble as long as thou live.' . . .

Later, Owein followed this route.

And Owein asked the way of the black man, and he told it. And Owein, like Cynon, followed the path till he came to beside the green tree, and he could see the fountain and the slab beside the fountain, and the bowl upon it; and Owein took up the bowl and threw a bowlful of water upon the slab. And thereupon, lo, the peal of thunder, and after the peal the shower. Greater by far were these than Cynon had said. And after the shower the sky lightened; and when Owein looked on the tree there was not one leaf upon it. And thereupon, lo, the birds alighting on the tree and singing. And even when Owein was most enraptured with the birds' song he could see a knight coming along the vale, and Owein received him and encountered him with spirit. And they broke their two lances, and drew their two swords and smote at each other, and thereupon Owein struck the knight a blow through his helm, both mail-cap and bourgoyne coif, and through skin, flesh and bone till it wounded the brain. And then the black knight knew that he had received a mortal blow, and turned his horse's head and fled. And Owein pursued him. But Owein could not get near enough to strike him with his sword, though he was not far off from him.

And thereupon Owein could see a great shining city. And they came to the gate of the city. And the black knight was let in, and the portcullis was let down upon Owein, and it struck him behind the hind-bow of the saddle, so that the horse was cut in two, right through him, and the rowels of the spurs close to Owein's heels, and so that the gate descended to the ground, and the rowels of the spurs and part of the horse outside, and Owein and the rest of the horse between the two gates. And the inner gate was closed, so that Owein might not get away; and Owein was in a quandary. And as Owein was thus, he could see through the join of the gate a road facing him and a row of houses either side of the road. And he could see a maiden with yellow curling hair, with a frontlet of gold on her head and a garment of yellow brocaded silk about her, and two buskins of speckled cordwain on her feet, and she coming towards the gate. . . .

The maiden gave timely assistance to Owein, then sheltered him in a house in the town. From here he watched the funeral of the noble owner of the castle, who died from the wounds received in the battle at the fountain.

And it seemed to Owein that the air rang, so great was the outcry and the trumpets and the clerics chanting. And in the middle of that host he could see the bier, and a pall of white bliant thereon, and wax tapers burning in great numbers around it, and there was not one man carrying the bier of lower rank than a mighty baron.

And Owein was certain that he had never beheld a train so beautiful as that with brocaded silk and satin and sendal. And following that host he could see a yellow-haired lady with her hair over her shoulders, and many a gout of blood on her tresses, and a torn garment of yellow brocaded silk about her, and two buskins of speckled cordwain upon her feet. And it was a marvel that the ends of her fingers were not maimed, so hard did she beat her two hands together. And Owein was certain that he had never beheld a lady as lovely as she, were she in her right guise. And louder was her shrieking than what there was of man and horn in the host. And when he beheld the lady he was fired with love of her, till each part of him was filled therewith. And Owein asked the maiden who the lady was. 'God knows,' said the maiden, 'a lady of whom it may be said that she is the fairest of women, and the most chaste, and the most generous, and the wisest and noblest. My mistress is she, and the Lady of the Fountain is she called, wife to the man thou slewest yesterday.' 'God knows of me,' said Owein, 'she is the lady I love best.' 'God knows,' said the maiden, 'She loves not thee, neither a little nor at all.' . . .

The maiden now set out to persuade the Lady of the Fountain to marry Owein.

'Thou knowest that thy dominions cannot be defended save by main strength and arms; and for that reason seek quickly one who may defend them.' 'How can I do that?' asked the countess. 'I will show thee,' said Luned. 'Unless thou canst defend the fountain thou canst not defend thy dominions. There is none can defend the fountain save one of Arthur's household; and I shall go,' said Luned, 'to Arthur's court. And shame on me,' said she, 'if I come away thence without a warrior who will keep the fountain as well or better than the man who kept it of yore.' 'That is not easy,' said the countess, 'but nonetheless go thou and put to the test that thou dost speak of.'

Luned set out under pretence of going to Arthur's court. And she came to the upper chamber to Owein; and there she remained along with Owein till it was time for her to have come from Arthur's court. And then she arrayed herself and came to see the countess. And the countess welcomed her. 'Thou hast news from Arthur's court?' asked the countess. 'The best news that I have, lady,' said she, 'is that I have prospered in my mission. And when wouldst thou have shown to thee the chieftain who has come with me?' 'Towards mid-day to-morrow,' said the countess, 'bring him to see me. And I shall have the town emptied against that time.'

And she came home. And towards mid-day on the morrow Owein put on a tunic and surcoat and a mantle of yellow brocaded silk, and a wide orfray of gold thread in the mantle, and two buskins of speckled cordwain on his feet, and the image of a golden lion fastening them. And they came to the countess's chamber; and the countess welcomed them. And the countess looked hard at Owein. 'Luned,' said she, 'this chieftain has not the look of a traveller.' 'What harm is there in that, lady?' asked Luned. 'Between me and God,' said the countess, 'that no man reft my lord's life from his body save this man.' 'All the better for thee, lady. Had he not been doughtier than he, he would not have taken his life. Nothing can be done in that affair,' said she, 'for it is over and done with.' 'Get you home,' said the countess, 'and as for me, I shall take counsel.'

And on the morrow the countess had the whole of her dominions summoned to one place, and she made known to them how her earldom was voided and might not be defended save by horse and arms and main strength. 'And I lay this choice before you: either do one of you take me, or let me take a husband from elsewhere who will defend it.'

They determined by their counsel to let her take a husband from elsewhere. And then she brought bishops and archbishops to her court to solemnize the marriage between her and Owein. And the men of the earldom did Owein homage. And Owein kept the fountain with spear and sword, dressed in black and on a pure black horse.

The six feaures of the challenge sequence are as faithfully reproduced in *The Lady of the Fountain* as in the description of the events at Nemi. The rainmaking charm indicates a cult site; the significant tree is present; the Black Knight defends the site with his life; there is a challenge involving a specific act; the victorious challenger takes over the defence of the site; and the new defender takes the position and wife of his predecessor. There is not much chance of accidental coincidence where six variables are involved. Unless the pattern of the story has been imported intact as a literary theme, we are witnessing here a recollection of the practice in Britain of the same cult as was in use at Nemi, with comparatively minor local variations.

The main difference between Classical descriptions of the practice at Nemi and *The Lady of the Fountain* is that the former are straightforward descriptions of a cult site in which the pagan nature of the activity is not concealed, whereas in the latter there is no reference to religion and the pattern of events has been given narrative form. This transformation into literature has had two noticeable effects on the 'challenge' as it appears in various episodes in the romances. One effect occurs because of a convention that a series of adventures was strung together as the actions of a single hero. When one of the adventures was the 'challenge', the 'continuation of the custom' had to be dropped to avoid immobilizing the hero. This is what happens later in *The Lady of the Fountain*, for after Owein has 'kept the fountain' for three years he is brought back to Arthur's court and further adventures. The other effect is that in a natural setting the lady must be given acceptable emotions. Her rapid change of allegiance from the slain to the slayer has to be toned down. She is therefore often described as oppressed by the defender so that his death is a welcome release, and a love interest on the part of the challenger may be introduced. In *The Lady of the Fountain*, narrative form has lengthened the story to give the lady time to make up her mind to marry Owein, but contrary to the general rule her love for the original defender is not concealed and the stark choice she faced is clearly stated. Unless she could provide for the defence of the fountain, her domains were insecure. She must take a husband who would defend it in single combat, and who better than the slayer of her previous lord?

Repetition of a remembered story inevitably results in omission; therefore, as well as sometimes being distorted, many incidents of the 'challenge' type are incomplete. But their pagan origin may still be discernible, as is evident from some of the examples in the following list of defenders of those typical cult sites – the river crossing, fountain, glade and island.

(a) Malgiers	li Gris, *or*			
(b) Maugys	(a black giant)	died defending a	bridge[14]	
(c) Esclados	le Ros	died defending a	fountain by a pine tree	
(d) An unnamed		knight died defending an	island	
(e) Marigart	le Rous	died defending a	glade which contained a pine	
(f) An unnamed	Black Knight	died defending a	tomb entrance	
(g) Balan,	a Red Knight,	died defending an	island	(Malory II 18)
(h) Iweret		died defending a	well by a lime tree[15]	
(i) Belias	le Noir	defended	the fountain of the two sycamores	(Sommer V 252/3 & 441)

The list as it stands shows merely the defence of a site appropriate for cult use. On its own, this is not definitive, for there could be a variety of reasons for these actions unconnected with religion. In the cases of (e), (f) and (h), there is a specific challenge, which may quicken interest; but three or four correspondences to the list of six identifying features may not be enough to convince. The case is different with the 'continuation of the custom' which has greater diagnostic weight than the challenge. Esclados in (c) took over the custom after killing the previous incumbent; Balan did the same; and Gawaine, the victor in (d), had to take the loser's place and to maintain the custom until the day his slayer should succeed to the office. In addition, Esclados married the previous defender's wife, and Gawaine took his lady and castle. There can be little doubt that in at least these two cases the incident is a parallel of *The Lady of the Fountain* in reflecting the events at Nemi. The less complete examples are likely to be eroded versions of the same, a natural result of the imperfection of oral tradition. Even they on occasion show secondary features which indicate their origin. The unnamed black knight in (f) had to guard his post all summer and winter, calling to mind the concentrated watchfulness of Frazer's King of the Wood. And the location of Belias's fountain – at the end of the Perilous Forest, towards the Waste Land – indicates that this situation is associated with pagan themes in other ways.

An interesting aspect of this group of defended sites is the wide variety within each identifying feature. The place may be a bridge, fountain, well, island, glade or tomb – all potentially cult sites and most of them, probably significantly, connected with water. The tree may be pine, lime, sycamore or, in *The Lady of the Fountain*, 'greener than the greenest fir'; and in contexts not mentioned here it is often a thorn. (The occurrence of sycamore is a puzzle, as according to botanists it was not introduced into Britain until the seventeenth century.) And the challenge may be made by striking a cymbal (or some other resonant object) hanging from the tree, or by blowing a horn. These variations could be the result of poetic embellishment, they could be accidental – the distinction between pine and thorn in French contexts is not very substantial – or they could represent minor local differences in an originating cult practice. We know that this sort of variation did occur in pagan sites, and apart from the egregious sycamore there is no obvious objection to the other variations falling into the category of local differences.

The list shows one interesting feature which is not mentioned in the sources from which Frazer compiled his description: the defender is often given a colour. Red and black predominate, grey occurs and so, in the combat at the ford between Pwyll and Hafgan, may white, for the latter's name has been glossed as Summer-White. Once again we have to choose between embellishment, accident and a local variation in a possible underlying cult practice – in this instance in a feature absent from the Classical prototype – and once again there seems no reason for choosing one rather than another except that when colour is used artificially – when, for instance, Beaumains challenges successively black, green, red and blue knights – the false note is at once apparent. We know that some colours had pagan significance. Red we shall find associated with cult figures; black has already been mentioned; white is associated with summer, grey perhaps with winter and green with spring. So there is at least no bar on these colours being associated with a pagan original.

To sum up, *The Lady of the Fountain* and the more complete examples in the list on p. 34 demonstrate that a tradition closely parallel to pagan practice at Nemi has given a number of episodes in the Arthurian cycle their shape. This tradition is strongest in 'the matter of Britain' but it is not confined to French sources, for it occurs in the *Mabinogion*, in the year-end battle between Pwyll and Hafgan at the ford. The large number of occurrences of the 'challenge', including incomplete examples – the list given above is far from exhaustive – indicates that this theme was an important constituent of the tradition underlying 'the matter of Britain', a tradition which we know was carrying other, undeniably pagan, material such as 'heads in wells' and, as described in the next chapter, annual kingship. It seems unlikely that an imported, purely literary motif should both capture such a large share of the British tradition and be the odd one out of three or four aspects of paganism in not being practised in Britain. There is therefore a good chance that the 'challenge' is a recollection of the acts of real men and women, that the strength of the tradition reflects the original power of the cult, and its variety, local differences at a number of sites.

2 Annual Kings

A feature of the 'challenge' emphasized by Frazer is the constant readiness of the defender, yet in one or two instances a fixed period is mentioned. Pwyll's fight at the ford took place at the year's end and a day, and in another case the task of defending a site was imposed for seven years. These fixed periods belong to a different sort of sacred kingship, though it is one which springs from the same pagan supposition as the challenge, that the well-being of a people and the fruitfulness of their husbandry depend on the vigour of their ruler. The principle is widespread. Frazer refers to sequences in which the 'divine king' died after one, three, eight and twelve years, sometimes by his own hand. For instance, in the province of Quilacare in Southern India,

according to an old traveller . . . there is . . . a Gentile house of prayer, in which there is an idol which they hold in great account, and every twelve years they celebrate a great feast to it, whither all the Gentiles go as to a jubilee. This temple possesses many lands and much revenue: it is a very great affair. This province has a king over it who has not more than twelve years to reign, from jubilee to jubilee. His manner of living is in this wise, that is to say: when the twelve years are completed, on the day of this feast there assemble together innumerable people, and much money is spent in giving food to Bramans. The king has a wooden scaffolding made, spread over with silken hangings: and on that day he goes to bathe at a tank with great ceremonies and sound of music, after that he comes to the idol and prays to it, and mounts on to the scaffolding, and there before the people . . . [after sundry mutilations] . . . he cuts his throat himself. And he performs this sacrifice to the idol, and whosoever desires to reign other twelve years and undertake this martyrdom for love of the idol, has to be present looking on at this: and from that place they raise him up as king.[16]

Frazer goes on to say, apropos annual kings:

That a king should regularly have been put to death at the close of a year's reign will hardly appear improbable when we learn that to this [i.e. Frazer's] day there is still a kingdom in which the reign and the life of the sovereign are limited to a single day.

37

There are two episodes in the romances which are reminiscent of some such pagan practice, but they concern a character who is closely connected with Arthur; a character, moreover, who is also associated with another pagan theme. In one of the 'challenges' listed on p. 34, (h), the successful challenger was Launcelot. The details are as follows:

Iweret of the Fair Forest Beforet lived in a valley of constant bloom with a wood which remained green both summer and winter. He demanded combat from any aspirant to his beautiful daughter's hand. Suitors had to go to a lime tree by a spring and strike a bell, which hung on the tree, three times, when Iweret would come out armed to meet them. Lanzelet made a challenge in this way and killed Iweret. The daughter, Iblis, readily forgave the death of her father and granted Lanzelet her hand and her estates. Later they married, and he became king of Iweret's country, Dodone.[17]

Since the challenger marries the daughter of the slain defender after a specific challenge at a spring with a significant tree nearby, this is a close match to the prototype. What are we to make of this association of Launcelot with a cult activity? And since this Launcelot is none other than Malory's Sir Launcelot de Lake, how are we to account for this description of the lover of Guenever as a married man? The answer to the second question effectively answers the first. It is that the Launcelot of the underlying tradition has an entirely different set of characteristics from the doughty champion of Arthur's court. Although a reader of Malory might conclude that no other knight is more completely integrated into the Arthurian Cycle, he would be wrong. Any connection Launcelot may appear to have with the post-Roman period is a result of 'naturalization'. What has happened is that Malory has suppressed the folk-lore and mythological aspects of Launcelot which clearly survive in 'the matter of Britain' and are in themselves a demonstration that the French poets relied on folk-tales for their themes. As a result of Malory's editorship, Launcelot's upbringing by a water-fay survives only in his descriptive title, 'of the Lake', and none of the episodes which identify his pagan origin are to be found in *Morte Darthur*. Launcelot is entirely a figure of 'the matter of Britain'. He is completely absent from early Welsh tales. But the original Launcelot was by no means a literary invention.

He was, the surviving accounts of his behaviour suggest, an embodiment of several pagan cults.

As well as being called 'of the Lake', Launcelot is associated with water in another way. In Sommer (IV 198) he is reported as cutting off a knight's head at the request of a woman, who threw the severed head into a well. The woman is not named, but she was the daughter or stepdaughter of a certain King Baudemagus (or Bagdemagus or Bandemagus), a name which identifies him, according to Newstead (p. 74 below), with the Welsh Bran. And Launcelot's father was King Ban, also identified by Newstead with Bran. These connections with a personage whom we now know to be the god of the cult of the severed head confirm the pagan significance of the episode and show that Launcelot was associated with the severed head cult, as well as the cult of sacred waters, the 'challenge' and, as we shall see, annual kingship.

The following story is told in *The High History of the Holy Grail*,[18] one of the elements of the 'matter of Britain':

The story saith that Lancelot went his way by strange lands and by forests to seek adventure, and rode until he found a plain land lying without a city that seemed to be of right great lordship. As he was riding by the plain land, he looketh toward the forest and seeth the plain fair and wide and the land right level. He rideth all the plain, and looketh toward the city and seeth great plenty of folk issuing forth thereof. And with them was there much noise of bag-pipes and flutes and viols and many instruments of music, and they came along the way wherein Lancelot was riding. When the foremost came up to him, they halted and redoubled their joy. 'Sir,' say they, 'Welcome may you be!' 'Lords,' saith Launcelot, 'Whom come ye to meet with such joy?' 'Sir,' say they, 'They that come behind will tell you clearly that whereof we are in need.'

Thereupon behold you the provosts and lords of the city, and they come over against Lancelot. 'Sir,' say they, 'All this joy is made along of you, and all these instruments of music are moved to joy and sound of gladness for your coming.' 'But wherefore for me?' saith Lancelot. 'That shall you know betimes,' say they. 'This city began to burn and melt in one of the houses from the very same hour that our king was dead, nor might the fire be quenched, nor never will be quenched until such time as we have a king that shall be lord of the city and of the honour thereunto belonging, and on New Year's Day behoveth him to be crowned in the midst of the fire, and then shall the fire be quenched, for otherwise may it never be put out nor extinguished. Wherefore have we come to meet you to give you the royalty, for we have been told that you are a good knight.' 'Lords,' saith Lancelot, 'Of such a kingdom have I no need, and God defend me from it.' 'Sir,' say they, 'You may not be defended thereof, for you come into this land at hazard, and great grief would it be that so good a land as you see this is were burnt and melted away by the default of one single man, and the lordship is right great, and this will be right great worship to yourself, that on New Year's Day you should be crowned in the fire and thus save this city and this great people, and thereof shall you have great praise.'

Much marvelleth Lancelot of this that they say. They come round him on all sides and lead him into the city. The ladies and damsels are mounted to the windows of the great houses and make great joy, and say the one to another, 'Look at the new king here that they are leading in. Now will he quench the fire on New Year's Day.' 'Lord!' say the most part, 'What great pity is it of so comely a knight that he shall end on such-wise!' 'Be still!' say the others. 'Rather should there be great joy that so fair city as this is should be saved by his death, for prayer will be made throughout all the kingdom for his soul for ever!' Therewith they lead him to the palace with right great joy and say that they will crown him. Lancelot found the palace all strewn with rushes and hung about with curtains of rich cloths of silk, and the lords of the city all apparelled to do him homage. But he refuseth right stoutly, and saith that their king nor their lord will he never be in no such sort. Thereupon behold you a dwarf that entereth the city, leading one of the fairest dames that be in any kingdom, and asketh whereof this joy and this murmuring may be. They tell him they are fain to make the knight king, but that he is not minded to allow them, and they tell him the whole manner of the fire.

The dwarf and the damsel are alighted, then they mount up to the palace. The dwarf calleth the provosts of the city and the greater lords. 'Lords,' saith he, 'Sith that this knight is not willing to be king, I will be so willingly, and I will govern the city at your pleasure and do whatsoever you have devised to do.' 'In faith, sith that the knight refuseth this honour and you desire to have it, willingly will we grant it to you, and he may go his way and his road, for herein do we declare him wholly quit.' Therewithal they set the crown on the dwarf's head, and Lancelot maketh great joy thereof. He taketh his leave and they commend him to God, and so remounteth he on his horse and goeth his way. . . .

This passage does not, like Frazer's report on the events at Quilacare, represent a first-hand account by a contemporary. If it refers to a system which involved limited kingship followed by the violent death of the king, many centuries of oral tradition separate the original from the earliest written form. Yet in several ways it conforms with remarkable exactness to the picture presented by Frazer. Kingship is emphasized; so is inevitable death: and death takes place on the first day of the year. Mary Williams[19] points out similarities to an account of annual kingship from Mexico in which the sacred king perished by fire. She also suggests that the Celtic year-end bonfires of Britain (at Hallowe'en) look as though they may originally have consumed a human victim. Of three aspects (in addition to a male ruler dying at the change to a new calendar period) to which she draws particular attention, two – music and public ceremony – are notable features of the events at both Quilacare and the Burning City. The third – an unblemished victim – is perhaps represented in native tradition by the 'comeliness' of a sacrificed youth in yet another episode involving Launcelot, shortly to be described. To these noteworthy features may be added the publicly expressed sorrow of the women. Annual public mourning for the dead year-god is mentioned in Babylonian texts;[20] the prophet Ezekiel saw the women of Jerusalem weeping for one such, Tammuz, at the north gate of the temple, and year after year Syrian women lamented the untimely fate of Adonis.[21]

With so many similarities between this adventure of Launcelot's and both established examples of limited kingship and the known attitudes of participants in ancient religious ceremonies, there seems to be a strong probability that oral tradition has here perpetuated a custom otherwise long forgotten in Britain and unmentioned by outside commentators on British prehistory.

The attempt to elect Launcelot to an annual kingship does not stand alone. Once again in the same romance this same knight is involved in what appears to be a sequence of deaths of crowned youths at annual intervals:[22]

Thereupon, Lancelot departeth from the hermitage and rideth on until he cometh forth of the forest, and findeth a waste land ... [In this barren land he finds a ruined city.] He entereth within and findeth the city all void of folk and seeth the great palaces fallen down and waste ... and the markets and exchanges all empty. He rideth amidst the streets and findeth a great palace that seemeth him to be better and more ancient than all the others. He bideth awhile before it and heareth within how knights and ladies are making great dole. And they say to a knight: 'Ha, God, sore grief and pity is this of you that you must needs die in such manner, and that your death may not be respited!' . . . Thereupon, lo you, the knight that cometh down into the midst of the hall, clad in a short red jerkin; and he was girt with a rich girdle of gold, and had a rich clasp at his neck wherein were many rich stones, and on his head he had a great cap of gold, and he held a great axe. The knight was of great comeliness and young of age. . . . 'Sir,' saith [Lancelot] to the knight, 'What is your pleasure?' 'Sir, needs must you cut me off my head with this axe, for of this weapon hath my death been adjudged. . .'.

Lancelot is persuaded to give his word to return to the city in a year's time to set his head in the same jeopardy. He then severs the head and hears a great cry far off in the city saying that he shall be avenged at the term set or before.

In due course Lancelot returned to the waste city on the appointed day, arriving at the hour of noon.[23]

In the city wherein Lancelot had arrived were many waste houses and rich palaces fallen down. He had scarce entered within the city when he heard a great cry and lamentation of dames and damsels, but he knew not on which side it was, and they say; 'Ha, God, how hath the knight betrayed us that slew the knight inasmuch as he returneth not. This day is the day come that he ought to redeem his pledge.' . . . [Launcelot avoided death by a hair's breadth and was told that the waste city would never again have been peopled of folk unless] a knight had come hither as loyal as you are. Full a score knights have arrived here by chance in the same manner as you came, and not one of them but hath slain a brother or a kinsman and cut off his head as you did to the knight, and each one promised to return at the day appointed; but all failed of their covenant . . . and so had you failed us in like manner to the others, we should have lost this city without recovery and the castles that are its appanages. [They lead Lancelot into the palace and hear presently] How the greatest joy in the world is being made in many parts of the forest, that was nigh the city. 'Sir,' say the damsels. 'Now may you hear the joy that is made of your coming. These are the burgesses and dwellers in the city that already know the tidings.' Lancelot leaneth at the windows of the hall, and seeth the city peopled of the fairest folk in the world, and great thronging in the broad streets and in the great palace, and clerks and priests coming in long procession praising God and blessing Him for that they may now return to their church, and giving benison to the knight through whom they are free to repair thither. Lancelot was much honoured throughout the city. The two damsels are at great pains to wait on him, and right great worship had he of all them that were therewithin and them that came thither, both clerks and priests.

This episode might easily be overlooked as perhaps being an eroded description of annual kingship. There is a series of beheadings at apparently yearly intervals but the royal status of the victim is not stated, nor is it made clear that the 'day appointed' was New Year's Day. Perhaps the costly ornaments and particularly the great cap of gold are the shadows of an original royalty. The matter must be left in doubt, but there is an interesting indication that the tenor of the passage is religious and pagan. The 'Waste Land' – the magical barrenness of the land, which could be averted by appropriate religious observances – is a common enough piece of pagan dogma. Add to this the human deaths at 'the day appointed' and there is an appreciable chance that the 'cry and lamentation of the dames and damsels', the joy of the dwellers in the city, and the 'clerks and priests coming in long procession' are the manifestations of what was originally a pagan annual festival at which a youth of 'great comeliness' went 'so graciously' – he was a willing sacrifice – to his death.

A third story that may be interpreted as having an origin in annual kingship concerns not Sir Launcelot but Sir Galahad, his son. The events that lead to Galahad's conception do not concern us here, but his mother was Elaine, King Pelles's daughter, and his father was Launcelot. Not all 'fathers' in the 'matter of Britain' are necessarily parents in the ordinary biological sense, but if we take Malory at face value Launcelot's father was King Ban, whose wife, Sir Launcelot's mother, was called Elaine, and Sir Launcelot's grandfather was King Launcelot. Apart from the obvious repetitions, there is an unexpected linking of the names in this family, for we learn from Malory (XI 3) that Sir Launcelot was originally named Galahad 'at the fountain stone' and only later confirmed as Sir Launcelot by the Lady of the Lake. This statement is extended in a French version (Sommer IV 176) by the comment that Sir Launcelot's father called him Galahad after his own father, who had the same name. Since the only grandfather of Launcelot whose name we know was King Launcelot, it may reasonably be assumed that he, exactly like Sir Launcelot himself, was originally called

	GALAHAD	was the original name of
had a son called	(King Ban)	
had a son called	GALAHAD	later renamed
had a son called	GALAHAD	

Galahad. The relationships of these names are summarized in the table above:

The repetition of the same names in successive generations is particularly noteworthy in conjunction with connections between the figures in this table and cult activity. It looks very much as if the repeated names are not to be considered as referring to individuals but to offices (such as, for example, 'dauphin'), but in some sense appropriate to pagan religion.

Sir Galahad's most conspicuous act of participation in a pagan cult activity is described in the following passage. The events took place in a city called Sarras (Malory XVII 22).

So at the year's end it befell that this King Estorause lay sick, and felt that he should die. Then he sent for the three knights [Galahad, Percivale and Bors] and they came afore him; and he cried them mercy of that he had done to them, and they forgave it him goodly; and he died anon. When the king was dead all the city was dismayed, and wist not who might be their king. Right so as they were in counsel there came a voice among them, and bade them choose the youngest knight of them three to be their king: For he shall well maintain you and all yours. So they made Galahad king by all the assent of the holy city, and else they would have slain him. And when he was come to behold the land, he let make above the table of silver a chest of gold and of precious stones, that hilled the Holy Vessel. And every day early the three fellows would come before it, and make their prayers.

Now at the year's end and the self day after Galahad had borne the crown of gold, he arose up early and his fellows, and came to the palace, and saw to-fore them the Holy Vessel, and a man kneeling on his knees in likeness of a bishop . . . [who said to Galahad,] 'Come forth the servant of Jesu Christ . . . I am Joseph of Arimathie . . . thou hast resembled me in two things; in that thou hast seen the marvels of the Sangreal, in that thou hast been a clean maiden, as I have been and am.'

And when he had said these words Galahad went to Percivale and kissed him, and commended him to God . . . And therewith he kneeled down to-fore the table and made his prayers, and then suddenly his soul departed to Jesu Christ, and a great multitude of

King	LAUNCELOT	who		
		who by	his wife	ELAINE
Sir	LAUNCELOT	who by	Pelles's daughter	ELAINE

angels bare his soul up to heaven, that the two fellows might well behold it. Also the two fellows saw come from heaven an hand, but they saw not the body. And then it came right to the Vessel, and took it and the spear, and so bare it up to heaven. Sithen was there never man so hardy to say that he had seen the Sangreal.

No recognizable account of a pagan custom could be expected to survive the automatic censorship of selection by clerics as a suitable subject to be written down in manuscript. It is therefore a vain hope that any reference to such a topic would be clear and unequivocal. Yet here in a well-known passage of a work which presents the scene as if it were bathed in the light of Christianity, the selection, rule and year-end death of a sacred king are spelled out with surprising clarity.

The original king died at the calendar YEAR END;
Galahad was made KING not of any ordinary kingdom, but of a HOLY city;
He reigned exactly ONE year;
At the YEAR'S END and the self day after he died.

The quotation from Malory has been given at some length to show how the significant details occupy only a small proportion of the text and yet appear to have been preserved intact. If they had been less overlaid by irrelevant material, and hence more obvious, they would not have survived.

We may sum up as follows the indications of cult activity associated with the Launcelots and Galahads:

Sir Launcelot cut off a head which was thrown into a well. (Sommer IV 198)
King Launcelot had his head cut off; it then fell into a well. (Sommer I 295)

In addition to the 'heads in wells':

Sir Launcelot took part in a 'challenge' in which he defeated the defender of a fountain.

Sir Launcelot was associated with the annual king of the Burning City.

Sir Launcelot was associated with the annual sacrifice at the Waste City.

Sir Galahad reigned for a year in the holy city.

Compared with other figures in the 'matter of Britain', Launcelot and Galahad show an outstanding wealth of pagan associations. Of the many references to severed heads, only a handful can be recognized from their context to be of cult significance, and of these the only two in which heads actually find their way into wells are those the 'Launcelots' appear in. And the only accounts of annual human deaths, unconnected with the challenge theme, are those mentioned above. It can therefore be reiterated with greater confidence that the Launcelots and Galahad stand out as prime cult figures. They and their associated activities are distinguished from the rest of the legends by a difference in origin; or else some special factor has produced exceptional clarity in the transmission of information about them from the remote times when the well cult, annual kingship and the challenge system were practised.

If the explanation given above of the last year of Galahad's life is correct, it raises the question why the death of a cult figure should coincide with the 'achievement' of the grail, a consummation never quite satisfactorily explained but clearly of the greatest spiritual significance. The elusive grail is typical of the legends as a whole in its variations in physical form, its supernatural associations and the wide range of interpretations that can be put upon it. It can be taken as fact, or imagination, or religious allegory or any mixture of the three. But is the religion in question Christianity, or some recollection of native paganism?

The grail is described in different sources as a cup, as a shallow dish, as a stoppered 'cruet' or even as an 'insignificant' stone. It is said, on the one hand, to be closely associated with Christ — either as a vessel used at the Last Supper or else as a receptacle in which His blood was collected as He was dying on the cross — and that it was brought to Britain by Joseph of Arimathea within a lifetime of Christ's death. On the other hand, a feature of the grail is the provision of sustenance in a way reminiscent of the magic vessels which were part of the religious paraphernalia of the Celts. There are also descriptions of ceremonies – obviously religious ceremonies – in which the grail is carried in a procession, but these take place in a castle and not, as one would expect of a Christian ceremony, in a consecrated building; and the grail-bearer is a woman and not a priest.

Oddest of all is the association of the grail with blood. Even in versions closely connected with Christianity, it is a receptacle for blood. In 'the matter of Britain', a spear drips blood into the grail; and on occasion a vessel (which, though not called by that name, takes the same place as the grail usually does in a ceremonial similar to the grail procession) is said to contain a severed human head surrounded by blood. What bearing, it may be asked, should the proposed identification of Galahad as an annual king, whose year-end death corresponds with what is otherwise known as 'the achievement of the grail', have on our acceptance of the wide range of descriptions of the grail? Clearly this much-discussed but still elusive object is a composite with associations deriving from widely different sources, and among its aspects are some which, like the link with annual kingship, could have an origin in cult activity. The question may therefore be restated as: 'Will this new information about Galahad enable cult motifs to be disentangled from the grail's other, more spiritual, associations, perhaps leaving the latter intact or even enhanced?' The second part of the question must be left to the individual reader to answer. The first part can be answered in the affirmative, and may in the process provide suggestions as to how some otherwise inexplicable aspects of the oral tradition came into being.

There is a large literature on the grail, and views on its significance are part of a larger discussion about the Celtic origins of the Arthurian cycle as a whole. Among the many opinions expressed, the one most relevant to our question is the view of R. S. Loomis in *The Grail. From Celtic Myth to Christian Symbol* that the grail does not fit properly into any form of Christian worship, either in its physical form or in its ritual use. On the other hand, in some of its aspects it has antecedents or parallels in Celtic myth. Let us see how this tallies with the grail in 'the matter of Britain' – in particular where Galahad is concerned.

Galahad is described, as are other princely youths who

47

attempt the grail quest, as proceeding through a series of strange adventures of a spiritual nature to the castle of Carbonek, which is the dwelling of the maimed king. There the seeker sees a procession in which, typically, a page carrying a white lance, from the point of which runs a drop of blood, is followed by two more pages carrying golden candel-abra with burning candles, then a maiden shining with a radiance which dims the candles and bearing the grail in her hands, and finally another maiden with a silver carving dish. The grail may on some occasions provide a ritual meal, on others food to correspond to the desires of everyone present or even sustenance for an indefinite period. It disappears mysteriously. The grail-bearer wears her arm in a sling at other times for, having touched the holy vessel, her hand cannot be used for ordinary purposes. The grail-seeker is not merely a spectator in the castle. He has a specific purpose in making the visit which, if his moral fibre is sufficiently tough to satisfy certain criteria, is to heal the maimed king either by asking a particular question or by anointing the sufferer with blood from the bleeding spear. This healing mission is a main, perhaps the sole, object of the grail quest.

In addition to any connection between the grail-seekers and the grail in the action of the story, Galahad more than other seekers was connected by his lineage with other personages who were prominent in the grail story. He is described as a lineal descendant of 'Joseph of Arimathea'; of Pelles, an inhabitant of the Grail Castle and himself a maimed king; and of the Fisher King, a name given to keepers of the grail and again a maimed king. Other grail-seekers are related to the dramatis personae of the story in rather different ways, but the same thread of relationship persists.

It seems, then, that there are two ways, action and lineage, by which tradition connects the grail with grail-seekers in general and Galahad in particular, as well as displaying both against a background of cult activity. We may now consider the way in which Galahad 'achieved' the grail. The salient features of this event seem to be that he died, and that the spear which dripped blood and a vessel which is elsewhere described as containing blood were present at the death. It is reasonable to suppose that these accessories were in some way connected with the ritual death of what has now been suggested to have been an annual king, so it is worth enquiring if there are any other incidents associated with this system which might shed some light on the mode of Galahad's death.

Usually when the grail appears, there is no ritual except the procession itself, which takes a variety of forms, all recognizable as variants of that already described. The grail is carried through the castle hall and disappears. As a result of its presence, magical phenomena such as the provision of plentiful food may take place, but the grail and its associated symbols are not generally used for any recognizable ritual purpose except the provision of a consecrated wafer for the father of the maimed king. In Malory XVII 20 & 21, however, the use of one of the symbols for a ritual purpose is described. Galahad is requested to use the blood provided by the spear that 'bled marvellously' to anoint the maimed king, who 'therewith clothed him anon and start upon his feet out of his bed a whole man'. What this may mean in terms of reality is difficult to guess, unless it reflects the widespread idea that the blood of a sacrificial victim has therapeutic powers, but the provision of blood for its healing qualities is interesting. It is an activity referred to elsewhere in the sequence of events which lead to Galahad's 'achievement' of the grail. One of the people who play an important part in the preparation of the hero for his task is Percival's sister. She accompanies him on his journey to the Castle of Carbonek where the grail is kept. On the way they are stopped by a group of knights who, having enquired if Percival's sister is a maiden, require her to yield to them the 'custom of the castle' which is that every passing maiden should fill a silver dish with blood from her right arm. The blood is to be used to anoint the lady of the castle who has suffered from a malady for many years. After some inconclusive fighting, Percival's sister willingly yields to the custom but bleeds so much that she dies. In due course she is buried at the holy city of Sarras 'in the spiritual place', unlike her three score predecessors, all of king's blood and twelve of them king's daughters who, having been martyred for the sick lady's sake, were buried at the castle.

In this episode, a chronically sick person of importance is purported to be healed by the application of blood from what sounds like a sacrificial victim who dies. This could be a parallel to the 'healing of the maimed king' which is the objective of the grail quest. And since, in final fulfilment of the quest, Galahad dies, the parallel might be extended to suggest that the bloody spear and blood-containing cup are not irrelevant to the death. For the victim's blood to have drained into the grail would provide a suitable original event to account for the various traditions in which a holy vessel contains blood.

All that has been said of annual kings up to now is that they died, being either burned or beheaded. This last instance, however, reveals the circumstances of the death in greater detail. A pagan ceremonial is described, and so is the ritual of death. There is a good chance that tradition has here preserved some previously unrecognized information about the past, and that the grail procession, Galahad's death and that of Percival's sister have their origin in actual historical events which took place more or less as described.

The grail, besides being frequently associated with blood, was supposed to provide sustenance in a general way. It was also used to hold the host or consecrated wafer which kept the maimed king's father alive. In this eucharistic version there is a possibility that blood was drunk from the cup and even flesh eaten from it. A figure who plays the part of the grail king, in a German version of the grail story, *Diu Crône*, drinks blood from a crystal goblet presented by a beautiful damsel[24] and on another occasion drinks three drops of blood from a jewelled salver, which Newstead equates with the grail. And in Malory, a 'host' – consecrated food for ritual eating – is said to be formed 'of fleshly man' (Malory XVII 20); while in the romance of Perlesvaus a certain King Gurguran, whose son had been killed by a giant, had the body cooked and divided the flesh among his people for them to eat. Ritual cannibalism is well known both from anthropological observations (Frazer's chapter 50 is called 'Eating the God') and from occasional archaeological finds of skulls with enlarged openings to facilitate extraction of the brain, and of skeletons bearing the marks of having been cut into joints before burial. The system must be looked on as a means of obtaining spiritual continuity with the deceased rather than as providing an addition to diet. This cult of the eaten god is that very system which Christ mercifully replaced and trans-muted into the sacraments of bread and wine, saying, 'Take, eat: this is my body.' And after the disciples had drunk from a cup of wine, 'This is my blood of the new testament, which is shed for many.'

Can we perhaps dissociate these bloody aspects of paganism from those interpretations of the grail which give it importance on account of its Christian associations? There seem to have been two false links. The first is a mistaken identification of the cult of the eaten god, as it appeared in later tradition, with the sacraments. The other concerns annual kingship, and the recollection of something as ephemeral as an emotion. It will be recalled that, in the description of annual kingship at the burning city, the hero was watched by the women of the city who for the most part said: 'Lord, what great pity is it of so comely a knight that he shall end on such-wise', while others said, 'Be still, rather should there be great joy that so fair a city as this should be saved by his death. . . .' It is not difficult to imagine that these feelings, expressed perhaps only in traditional tales and therefore not an active cult, should have struck a chord in the hearts of early Christians in Britain. Such a muddled mistaken identification of Christianity with paganism could have been the origin of a group of traditions, which are otherwise difficult to explain, to the effect that Christianity arrived early to the British Isles; that Bran, who was one of the gods in whose names these cruelties were perpetrated, brought Christianity to Britain; and that the holy vessel which had been used at the Last Supper, or had held Christ's blood, had been fetched to Britain by 'Joseph of Arimathea' in the first century A D. Such fantasies had their effect on real life when British bishops claimed precedence over their continental counterparts on account of the supposed earlier conversion of their country.

If the conclusion that the grail was originally a cult symbol is correct, then it follows that the bringer of the grail has been wrongly identified as Joseph of Arimathea, perhaps through some now forgotten resemblance of name or symbolism. The figure to whom that name is given in the Arthurian cycle can originally have had nothing to do with Christianity, for he was a maimed king – stricken through the thigh by a sword (Malory XVII 19). From this conclusion it also follows that the traditions which describe the bringing of the grail and the ritual fish meal which gave the Fisher King or Rich Fisher his name, may have their origins in religious innovations and pagan dogmas from a remote past. The synopsis of the relevant material which follows is offered without comment. The extent to which, divested of its Christian connotations, it reads as a recollection of real events is left to the reader to decide.

Joseph was the original possessor of the grail. The story begins when, with his sister and her husband Bron, he left his home in an eastern country and, taking the grail with him, dwelt for a long time in foreign lands. In obedience to a celestial command he there set up a special table for the service of the grail, with a eucharistic function in mind. On this table was placed the holy vessel and opposite to it a fish, specially caught by Bron who on account of this activity was known as the Rich Fisher. Clean-living believers who sat at the table enjoyed a miraculous plenty.

At the table was a seat specially reserved for an as yet unborn descendant of Bron. Any unqualified user of the seat perished, either swallowed up by the ground or else seized up to the skies by fiery hands.

Bron had twelve sons, eleven of whom married; but the remaining, celibate, brother Alain was their leader. He was in due course to have a male heir who would play an important part in the grail story.

A party including Bron, with the grail, and Alain was despatched to find a new home in the west, in the Vales of Avaron (which turned out to be Glastonbury) and there to await the prophesied heir. Later they were joined by Joseph himself, who at his death committed the grail to Alain. Alain, who then became known as the first of the Fisher Kings, took it to the oddly named 'Terre Foraine' where Galaphes built the Castle of Corbenic – Malory's Carbonek or Corbin – to contain the holy vessel. There successive guardians, also called Fisher Kings or Rich Fishers, awaited the coming of the successful grail-seeker.

While the hero was awaited, the land was under an enchantment. The normal abundance of nature was supposed to be vitiated by the magical effect of the disabling wound that the maimed ruler had suffered. In course of time the expected hero arrived, and by his dedication to his task reversed this effect. The maimed king was said to be healed, and the land regained its prosperity.

3 The Dolorous Stroke

In *Morte Darthur* the Dolorous Stroke was delivered by Balin le Savage against King Pellam. Using the marvellous spear which dripped blood into the grail in the grail procession, Balin smote Pellam so that he

fell down in a swoon, and therewith the castle roof and walls brake and fell to the earth, and Balin fell down so that he might not stir foot nor hand. And so the most part of the castle, that was fallen down through that dolorous stroke, lay upon Pellam and Balin three days. . . .

And King Pellam lay so, many years sore wounded, and might never be whole till Galahad the haut prince healed him in the quest of the Sangreal. . . . [Meanwhile Balin left the castle and] rode forth through the fair countries and cities, and found the people dead, slain on every side. And all that were alive cried, O Balin, thou hast caused great damage in these countries; for the dolorous stroke thou gavest unto King Pellam three countries are destroyed, and doubt not but that vengeance will fall on thee at the last. (Malory II 15 & 16)

There are five ways in which this passage and versions of it reflect paganism:

1 The striker is Balin, who can be argued to be a god.
2 In the grail procession, the weapon appears in what seems to be a religious ritual.
3 The recipient of the blow is a type of sacred king.
4 The effect of the blow is to cause destruction and barrenness.
5 This barrenness is reversible by human sacrifice and the ritual application (or possibly consumption) of the victim's blood.

The key to understanding the Dolorous Stroke lies in item (4). This shows once again the supposition, that the bodily well-being of a king affected the prosperity of his people, which has served to explain the 'challenge' and annual kingship. The idea of magical barrenness occurs in both

Welsh tradition and the 'matter of Britain', often in the latter being described as the Waste Land. It has already been encountered here in the waste city, where there were 'great palaces fallen down and waste . . . and the city all void of folk'. This condition was reversed when Launcelot presented himself for year-end beheading and the city and palaces once again became thronged with people.

In another version, the Waste Land, occurring because King Labor – the father of the maimed king – had been killed by a 'Saracen' king with a magic sword, is described as follows:

And it was in the land of Logris; and so befell great pestilence and great harm to both realms. For sithen increased neither corn, nor grass, nor well-nigh no fruit, nor in the water was no fish; wherefore men call it the lands of the two marches, the waste land, for that dolorous stroke. (Malory XVII 3)

And Loomis mentions another example in a tale from the 'matter of Britain' in which, as a result of a wound to the Fisher King the land of Logres fell under an enchantment, so that neither peas nor wheat were sown, no children were born, marriages did not take place, plants and trees did not turn green and birds and animals did not reproduce, 'so long as the king was maimed' (Loomis 279).

There are instances from outside the 'matter of Britain' of the magical barrenness of the land and of the incapacity to rule of a king who was not whole, but the examples given above are exceptionally clear statements of the supposed relationship between these two factors. This ties in with the presence in the 'matter of Britain' of sacred kings of the challenge type and of kings who ruled for fixed periods, for these systems would have the effect of providing a vigorous ruler. On the basis of the tenet outlined above this would seem both logical and desirable, as it would tend to promote prosperity.

One obvious way in which the vigour of a ruler would become apparent would be in his capacity for procreation. This requirement occurs in the story of Alan, king of Brittany, of whom Walter Map reported about AD 1200 that in the parish where he was castrated 'no animals even today can bring forth young, but, when ripe for bearing, they go outside the parish to deliver their offspring' (Loomis 280). And, in

Welsh tradition, the men of Dyfed were unhappy that their lord, Pwyll, should be childless, so:

they summoned him to them. The place where they met was Preseleu* in Dyfed. 'Lord,' said they, '. . . our fear is lest thou have no offspring of the wife thou hast; and so, take another wife of whom thou mayest have offspring. Thou wilt not last for ever,' said they, 'and though thou desire to remain thus, we will not suffer it from thee.'[25]

There need be no surprise, therefore, that impotency in a king should be a form of lack of vigour much to be feared. Such a supposition would account for the nature of the wound suffered by the maimed king which was so severe as to cause general barrenness. A wound in the genitals is specifically referred to only in the case of Anfortas, the equivalent in *Parzival* of Chrétien de Troyes's Fisher King. But the frequent description of a wound as being between or through the thighs in connection with other instances of maimed kings is generally thought to refer to emasculation. Among the better known figures to have received this wound are King Pellinore, who was wounded between the thighs in a boat; Percival's father, who was wounded through the legs and as a result suffered poverty; Pelles, to whom Malory attributes the same adventure as is related above of Pellinore; and the Fisher King, who in 'Percival le Gallois' is said to have maimed himself through the legs.

The repetition of this motif in a group of individuals who are linked together in other ways in the 'matter of Britain', and the way in which impotency is set in opposition to general prosperity, suggest that a facet of pagan thinking has survived into the era of the written word. A doctrine of this type would appear to give no warrant for the castration of real human sacred kings. It could be expected to have the opposite effect, and to encourage taboos to prevent such a mutilation from occurring by accident to a sacred king. This seems a far cry

---

*The source of the bluestones of Stonehenge, here called Preseleu but shown on modern maps as Prescelly, has generally been assumed to have some special significance. It is therefore interesting to find it associated in tradition with Pwyll, a character who has other links with paganism: his name 'Head of Annwn' (the Otherworld); his year-long rule, culminating in the battle at the ford; his wife, whose name Rhiannon signifies 'great queen' – an appropriate appellation for a goddess – and who, according to Ross,[26] is an insular equivalent of the Continental Epona, the goddess of a horse cult.

from the Classical examples of ritual castration in which, as in the worship of Astarte in Syria, for instance,[27] the priests were eunuchs and wore women's attire and ornaments after they had castrated themselves at a public festival. There, the motif of sacred kingship is absent, and so is the supposed link with natural abundance. But one factor in the Classical account, self-mutilation, may not be irrelevant to British paganism, for on one or two occasions the wound is said to be self-inflicted. In general, however, there is no reflection in British tradition of the honouring of the goddess by the voluntary revocation of manhood by her priests. Here, it seems, there was thought to be a balance of magical forces in which the deficiency on the part of the ruler was resisted by sacrifice or overcome by the election of temporary kings who were replaced before their vigour waned. Though there is a hint that castration may have been the lot of one type of sacred king whose reproductive function might be considered dispensable once he had mated with the woman who represented the goddess.

The Dolorous Stroke took place in the Grail Castle, the Maimed King was usually resident there, and the grail procession took place there. Since all these activities, whether factual or not, can be interpreted as having their origin in paganism, the Grail Castle itself and any of the other activities that took place there may have a similar origin. We are told of the Grail Castle that it was constructed by Galaphes (or Alphisem or Alphasan, as he became known after 'baptism'), who was king of the Terre Foraine which, when the Dolorous Stroke was struck, became the Terre Gaste, i.e., the Waste Land. It was to the Terre Foraine that Alain came with the grail after Joseph's death. Here Galaphes was cured of a normally fatal disease and ordered the construction of the castle of Corbenic, otherwise known as the 'adventurous palace', to hold the grail and as a residence for the line of grail-keepers (also called Fisher Kings) which started with Alain.

The Grail Castle was a dangerous place; 'thereafter came many a knight who wished to tarry there, but without fail none tarried there but was found dead in the morning'.[28] Galaphes/Alphisem himself was wounded to the death when he attempted to spend a night in the castle he had himself built and was struck between the thighs by a 'fiery man'. We know little else about Alphisem except that, under the name Galaphes (or something not much different), he had a connection with an important event in the prehistory of religion. But here in the 'fiery man' is another potential contact with pagan matters. In close parallels of this incident, the 'fiery man' with a spear is replaced by a flaming lance which operated without human agency, or by a lance with a flaming pennon. The flaming weapon in tales of this kind often represents the lightning or its close companion, the thunderbolt. Thor with his hammer is by no means the only local equivalent of Zeus. In other instances the lightning weapon may be a stone, an axe, a sword, a spear, or even an iron bar. In the present context of Galaphes and the other night-adventurers in the Grail Castle, the flaming weapon finds its closest parallels in Irish literature. There the flaming sword and flaming spear are described in a way which relates them to the Welsh god Beli.[29]

The individuals who play leading parts in the events described as happening in the Grail Castle fall into two main categories. There are the grail-keepers – limited in their movement by their wounds, sometimes restricted to the fireside or confined to bed; and the grail-seekers – extremely active, spirited fighters and wanderers in search of adventure. The latter are often said to be the descendants of kings who have the titles Fisher or Maimed or 'of the Waste Land'. They include the three successful contenders, Galahad, Percival and Bors, and, in (for once) unsuccessful roles, such famous names as Launcelot and Gawaine. The seekers in the course of their wanderings often find themselves in circumstances which test not only their martial ardour but also their spiritual qualities. One such is the night adventure of the perilous bed in the Grail Castle. As its name implies, the perilous bed, like the perilous seat at the grail table, is a position of great danger. The occupant of it is exposed to a severe wound by means which are largely independent of human agency. What happened to Gawaine in the Castle of Corbenic is described in Sommer (IV 342) as follows: after having been welcomed, Gawaine was seated by the king.

While they were talking, a white dove carrying a censer entered the hall and disappeared in one of the rooms. Sweet odours filled the whole place. All present knelt in reverence. The tables were laid. Gawain wondered what it all meant, and sat down with the others.

57

A most beautiful damsel issued from the room which the dove had entered, carrying a rich vessel. She held the vessel high above her head. All who saw it bowed their heads except Gawain, who did not understand its signification. Gawain paid attention only to the damsel's great beauty. Those whom the damsel passed devoutly knelt down. The tables were filled with the most delicious food, and sweet odours pervaded the place. Gawain's eyes were riveted on the damsel until she departed. While all had their fill of what they most desired, Gawain had nothing. After the meal all rose and left the palace; when Gawain wanted to do likewise, he found the gates locked. . . . Seeing a beautiful bed, Gawain was going to lie on it when a damsel told him not to enter the Adventurous Bed without arms, and showed him some. After arming himself, Gawain sat down on the bed. A flaming lance entered the room and struck Gawain. Its point penetrated his shoulder; he swooned. When he regained consciousness, he felt that someone invisible drew back the lance. Sorely wounded, he remained on the bed until it was dark. . . . [More adventures followed. Gawain was attacked by a dreadful serpent and by an armed man. There was a thunderstorm, and the palace shook. Finally,] the beautiful damsel of the previous evening came to the middle of the place, placed the holy vessel on a silver table surrounded by twelve censers [and the voices of angels sang a heavenly song]. After a little while the damsel carried the vessel back, and the singing ceased. Darkness descended on the palace, but Gawain felt that he was healed.

As R. S. Loomis points out in *Arthurian Tradition and Chrétien de Troyes*, the French romances have 'preserved for us the wind, the slamming windows, the thunder and the fiery lance which betray the presence of the storm god'.[30] And since Launcelot too is the subject of a night attack by a fiery lance in a testing bed (Sommer IV 166), once again an episode with its origin in paganism is attributed to this particular knight.

The adventure of the perilous bed is sometimes preceded by and sometimes followed by a ride in a wheeled vehicle. The best known instance concerns Sir Launcelot, in whose story the episode must at one time have had a now forgotten significance, for Chrétien's *Lancelot* is subtitled 'Le Chevalier de la Charrette' – the Knight of the Cart. The incident which gave him this unlikely title is told in rather different ways by Malory and Chrétien. In *Morte Darthur*, Queen Guenever called together ten knights with their ladies and attendants, and one May morning 'they rode a-Maying in woods and meadows as it pleased them, in great joy and delights'

(Malory XIX 1). Unfortunately Sir Meliagrance, who entertained a secret affection for the queen, noticed that the knights who accompanied her were unarmed, being 'arrayed in green for Maying . . . bedashed with herbs, mosses and flowers'. He then sent a force of armed men to capture the queen and her party. Guenever was able to send a message to Sir Launcelot, but Meliagrance saw the messenger depart and, guessing to whom he had been sent, set an ambush. As a result, Launcelot found himself with his horse slain and, being encumbered with armour, unable to continue on his mission to rescue the queen. He therefore requisitioned a cart belonging to Meliagrance and compelled the driver to take him to the place where the queen was imprisoned. There he forced an entry and obtained the queen's release.

In Chrétien's *Lancelot*, a strange knight dares King Arthur to let the queen be the prize for the winner of a combat. The knight – who we later learn to be Meleagant (the equivalent in Chrétien of Malory's Meliagrance or Meliagaunce) – defeats Arthur's champion, so the queen becomes his captive. In pursuit of her Launcelot takes the ride in the cart, though not without some hesitation on account of the demeaning nature of this vehicle. In it, he proceeds to a castle where he undergoes successfully the test of the perilous bed and of the flaming lance. Later, after adventures which include a battle at a ford and a year-end challenge to single combat, he kills Meleagant and so disposes of the threat to the queen.

This description of the ride in the cart seems a reasonable enough picture of a determined man in heavy armour wishing to travel further and faster than he would have been able to do on foot. Even his hesitation seems natural enough, but it elicits an odd explanation from Chrétien de Troyes, who 'says of towns where there were many carts in his time, that there was but one each in the time of his hero, and that it was used to carry malefactors through the streets previous to their being executed. Thus, to be seen in a cart was then much the same as to be pilloried in later times; and it was, according to him, unlucky even to meet a cart.'[31] So, wishing to excuse his hero's reluctance to enter the demeaning cart, Chrétien had recourse to the description of a past which was presumably unfamiliar to his readers, culminating in the apparently nonsensical notion that at one time it was bad luck even to meet a cart.

It is impossible to guess what effect this would have had on twelfth-century readers. Obviously carts would have been an ordinary means of transport from time immemorial, and even if a recollection had persisted of a period when wheeled vehicles were scarce, they would have been remembered as the prized possessions of a warlike aristocracy or even the appurtenances of deities (there is not the same distinction between the words cart and chariot in French as there is in English). We know that vehicles were still in use for ritual purposes in Western Europe in the later stages of paganism. Tacitus describes an example in the first century in northern Germany. Beyond the Langobardi (probably beyond the Elbe) and stretching into the darkest north of Germany come the Reudigni, Aviones, Anglii, Varini, Eudoses, Suardones, and Nuithones.

These tribes are protected by forests and rivers, nor is there anything noteworthy about them individually, except that they worship in common Nerthus, or Mother Earth, and conceive her as intervening in human affairs, and riding in procession through the cities of men. In an island of the ocean is a holy grove, and in it a consecrated chariot, covered with robes: a single priest is permitted to touch it: he interprets the presence of the goddess in her shrine, and follows with deep reverence as she rides away drawn by cows: then come days of rejoicing, and all places keep holiday, as many as she thinks worthy to receive and entertain her. They make no war, take no arms: every weapon is put away; peace and quiet are then, and then alone, known and loved, until the same priest returns the goddess to her temple, when she has had her fill of the society of mortals. After this the chariot and the robes, and, if you are willing to credit it, the deity in person, are washed in a sequestered lake: slaves are the ministrants and are straightway swallowed by the same lake: hence a mysterious terror and an ignorance full of piety as to what that may be which men only behold to die.[32]

The two types of use of wheeled vehicles, the aristocratic and the religious, are attested by archaeology to have been widespread and are the only likely influences to have penetrated from the time when carts were scarce into traditional tales. How is it, then, that Chrétien seems to be saying the exact opposite by referring to the early use of carts as demeaning and shameful?

One possible solution to this problem is that the divergence is more apparent than real. There is a good fit between what

Chrétien says and what we know of the pagan use of wheeled vehicles. At a time in the past beyond the recollection of his readers when carts were limited to one per town, Chrétien's 'unlucky even to meet' matches very well the way in which a pagan ritual vehicle, such as the chariot of Nerthus covered over in its island grove, might have been recollected in the oral tradition. The reference to human death is equally apposite to paganism, and we know that criminals were on occasion used as sacrifices. There are, then, three ways in which Chrétien's comments on the cart fit the assumption that they have an origin in paganism: the singularity of vehicles, their awesomeness and their connection with human death. In addition, the circumstances in which the cart is to be found, carrying a victim to and from the night adventure in the perilous bed in the Grail Castle, may be explained by reference to pagan originals; and the individuals who are said to ride in the cart have associations with paganism in other respects. There is, therefore, a substantial possibility that the descriptions of heroes riding in carts in the 'matter of Britain' have their origin in a ritual which actually took place in Britain. The details of this ritual are better preserved in stories in which Bors or Gawaine is the hero. The latter (Sommer IV 347), when he had recovered from being wounded in the perilous bed by a flaming spear, was seized by the arms and legs and carried from the hall into an outside yard, where he was bound to a cart and left until dawn. Then an old woman with a scourge drove the cart through the town. There were minstrels, and the victim was exposed to the taunts of the populace, and was pelted with mud, dung and old shoes. After having been escorted out of the town and over a bridge, he was freed by the old woman.

That Chrétien should attribute hesitation to the hero who was embarking on such an adventure as has been outlined above is understandable, even though the author was dealing with what had become merely an entertaining story, so divorced from its original that the victim is recorded as surviving undamaged. It may be supposed that in the underlying reality of a thousand years or more earlier he suffered a starker fate. But, though the individual may have perished, the office would have continued, with a new holder.

The word hero is appropriate in describing the selfless youth who, for the benefit of the community, embarks on

'adventures' in which he is foredoomed to death or to
wounding and shameful treatment. The dictionary definition
of the hero of antiquity – a man of superhuman qualities
favoured by the gods; partly divine being, son of god and
mortal, or deified man – could aptly be used of our Western
seekers after adventure in a pagan milieu. The latter, indeed,
entered folk tradition from a society in a stage of development
which bears some resemblance to that which produced the
hero-tales of ancient Greece. The description 'semi-divine' is
sometimes used of the personages of human origin who in
myths play the part of deities, but this is self-contradictory.
The ways men could earn the title of hero in the service of
pagan gods have been brought to light by the analysis of the
'matter of Britain' given above, in which the earthly participants clearly stay human to their predetermined ends.
Curiously to modern ears, these Western heroes did not
depend entirely on their personal prowess. Conception and
birth were also important factors in the making of the heroes
of the Celtic literatures of Wales and Ireland.[33] A similar
tendency may be observed in the 'matter of Britain'. Birth
must have been of importance in choosing the participants
when the grail-seeker is said to be close kin to the grail-bearer
and to the beheaded victim. The position is somewhat
confused by the presence in the pages of the 'matter of Britain'
of a number of deities masquerading as the kings and queens
whose 'children' play the parts of heroes and their female
equivalents. Since conception and birth, like dismemberment
and death, imply real flesh and blood, we are concerned with
human parenthood and, in so far as this may have had
religious significance in pagan times, with whether there are
incidents in the 'matter of Britain' which could have owed
their origin to copulation as a ritual act.

When viewed against the general background of cult
activity in connection with the adventures of grail-seekers,
there are two incidents which might fall into this category.
One is the story of how Launcelot, unwillingly, became the
father of Galahad, being deceived on the girl's father's
instructions. The deliberate intention to produce a hero as a
result of this union is quite clearly stated. 'And for this intent:
the king knew well that Sir Launcelot should get a child upon
his daughter, the which should be named Sir Galahad the
good knight, by whom all the foreign country should be

brought out of danger, and by him the Holy Grail should be achieved.' (Malory XI 2) The place in which this plan was made (though it was executed in a nearby castle called Case) is the Castle of Corbenic, where the Dolorous Stroke took place, and the king is Pelles, himself a 'maimed king' smitten 'through both the thighs' (XVII 5). It is reasonable enough to construe the bedding of Elaine as an act which, by emphasizing procreation and fertility, was supposed to counterbalance the sterility implied by the wound between the thighs. The begetting of Galahad is presented by Malory as a more or less isolated incident, but a similar situation which resulted in the conception of Helain le Blanc suggests that there may have been a prelude, and that this type of behaviour follows naturally after another activity typical of contenders to sacred kingship – personal success in combat.

Helain's conception is described in Sommer (IV 259ff). The scene is set when King Brangoire summons a large number of knights to a tournament at the Castle de la Marche* in order to celebrate the anniversary of his coronation. The reward offered is that the best knight will be seated in a golden chair at a table reserved for himself and twelve others who have distinguished themselves in the tournament. He will be entitled to choose for himself the most beautiful damsel from among those present, and twelve others for the twelve knights at the table. In the event (Sommer IV 264), Bohort – otherwise known as Bohors or Bors, a grail-seeker who has been brought up by the Lady of the Lake – is duly chosen by the ladies as the bravest and most handsome knight. He is attended by the king's daughter (who is, it need scarcely be said, the most beautiful damsel there) and is seated in the special seat, which causes him to blush. The king then informs him that he can take the most beautiful damsel for himself, with her wealth and position, and that it is his duty to select the other twelve damsels according to an old custom of the country which has invariably been followed by both the king and his forebears throughout the duration of their lives. After a feast, the damsels are presented to the knights, but to everyone's surprise Bohort refuses the hand of

---

* Marche means boundary. In Celtic times, physical boundaries had a significance comparable to the boundary between one day and the next (the witching hour), and one year and the next (at that time, Hallowe'en). However, in the Castle of the Marche the word is as likely to mean the boundary between the real world and the otherworld as a physical boundary.

the princess because he is dedicated to the quest for the grail, success in which requires him to preserve his virginity. The evening's entertainment continues, however, with caroling (the original meaning of carol being a round dance) and dancing until late, after which Bohort sleeps in a bed of honour in a room by himself. This arrangement clearly contradicts the stated intention of the tournament, which is that the victor should marry the princess and become lord of the country. Recourse is therefore had to a magic ring, by which means the union of the princess and the virgin grail-seeker is brought about and so Helain le Blanc is conceived. Since 'magic' is used to bring about not marriage but copulation and conception, it may reasonably be inferred that these are the real underlying (but unstated) objectives of the tournament.

If the reference to 'anniversary' is taken to imply an annual event, then we should expect to find the picture presented above, of the honoured and procreative victor, complemented by that of the same individual vanquished and shamed. Perhaps that is why Bohors is also recorded, on a day of festival in mid-August, as being driven through the streets of a town (Roevent or Carawent en Gales) in the shameful cart with his legs tied to the shafts and his hands tied behind his back, while the population throw filth and old shoes at him.

There is a strong resemblance between the events at the Castle de la Marche, leading to the conception of Helain, and the conception of Galahad. Both fathers, Bohort and Launcelot, were brought up by the Lady of the Lake (Sommer IV 218); the fathers of the girls, Pelles and Bran (of which latter name Brangoire is likely to be a compound), were Fisher Kings; the name Elaine, without a terminal e if masculine and with or without an h at the beginning indiscriminately, is used several times in connection with each set of participants; and there is a specific intention, stated or unstated, to produce a grail-contender by the union of the parties. It is suggested that this act, a deliberate demonstration of fecundity, could have its origin in the pagan principle that behaviour of this sort would tend to promote prosperity. And it will later be suggested that the personal names of the major figures in the background of these events – Bran, the Lady of the Lake, and Pelles – have their origin in pagan cults and probably represent pagan deities. With this

64

in mind, the comparison between the events planned by Pelles at Corbenic and those which took place at the Castle de la Marche will be seen to be very close. In each case, the male representative of a goddess meets the female representative of a god to conceive a hero. But this close similarity does not necessarily mean that there was only one 'castle' and one set of personages in the originating situation. Uniformity stemming from a central authority is unlikely to have been the rule in prehistory, so local variations in both time and place are likely to have resulted in the same dogma producing different but recognizably related patterns of fulfilment.

There is one more type of story from the 'matter of Britain' in which sexuality and grail-seekers come together. In a couple of instances connected with Avalon – a name which for other reasons may be argued to represent a cult site – the hero's lovemaking is interrupted by men with axes, or, more particularly, jusarms or gysarms (a sort of poled axe). The close relationship of these incidents to what has been discussed above suggests that they too should be regarded as possibly having their origin in recollected paganism. In one the hero is Gawaine and his partner the king of Cavallon's sister. She is kissing him and making great joy when they are attacked by men with axes and jusarms. In the other the hero is Gareth, Gawaine's brother, and his partner the lady Lionesse, whom Gareth has rescued from the Red Knight of the Red Laund (or glade) after a combat following a challenge which consisted of blowing a horn hanging from a sycamore tree. Later, she comes to Gareth's bed in the hall of her brother's castle in the Isle of Avilion. While they are kissing, a knight appears with a long gisarm in his hand. In the ensuing combat Gareth receives a severe wound in the thigh (Malory VII 22).

This brings to an end the list of episodes from the 'matter of Britain' which appear likely to have an origin in native paganism. Whether the individual incidents are in some cases derived from the real past cannot be said with certainty. But the element of probability may be quite substantial in, for instance, the Challenge, where the original situation (known from Classical reports) is accurately described and the correspondence covers a number of factors. For other incidents, taken on their own, the degree of probability may be much smaller if the picture of the past we are comparing them with is more a matter of inference and if the correspondence covers fewer factors. Taken together, however, the repetition of several themes which are known to have occupied pagan minds does firmly suggest that the explanation of an origin in paganism for certain themes in the 'matter of Britain' is correct.

It is also possible to speculate on the extent to which the repetition of ancient themes carries with it previously un-recognized information about the remote past. The answer is bound to be a guess, but if the guess is made according to approved guidelines it will not be irrelevant. First, any factors which are found to be repeated in different contexts are to be noted; then, in as compact a manner as possible, a model of the past should be imagined – a purely theoretical recon-struction – which will best explain the form of the observed end-product, the written word as it appears in Chrétien, in Sommer, and ultimately in Malory. Such a model will hold the field until such time as it is replaced by another which is a better fit to the observed facts.

If we are to construct such a model we must begin with the single unifying factor which underlies the whole spectrum of pagan behaviour outlined in the pages above: that is, the supposition that virility in a king promotes the prosperity of a country. The result of this supposition is that tradition is permeated by references both to prosperity and to its feared imaginary antithesis. Thus, the king of the Waste Land is also the 'very rich Fisher King' and as such emblematic of abundance; and the queen of the Waste Land is also 'called the queen of most riches in the world' (Malory XIV 1). From this aspect of paganism stem such features of the 'matter of Britain' as:

The Rich Fisher, the Fisher Kings (which have suffered verbal degeneration in Malory to King Pescheour or lord Petchere), the Waste Land and its kings and queens, the waste city where annual kingship was practised, and descriptions of magical barrenness in general.

One of the ways in which virility could be demonstrated was by fecundity. Here again negative aspects have survived better, so to the lovemaking which resulted in the conceiving of heroes is opposed the ideal of male virginity set for grail-seekers and the threat of the magical effects of castration implied in the wound between the legs. Hence:

The amours arranged at the Grail Castle, and at the castles of la Marche and the Isle of Avilion; the virginity of successful grail-seekers; the maimed and languishing kings of the Grail Castle and other castles; the kings and heroes wounded through the thigh; the Dolorous Stroke.

The success of a sacred king in encouraging abundance would, if it depended on his virility, clearly decline as he grew old and infirm. Systems were therefore adopted which led to his replacement while still young and strong, either by a trial of strength or by limiting the period of kingship. The first of these alternatives was initiated by a formal challenge, after which there was a fight to the death. The loser was decapitated and his head either thrown into a well or else exposed on a stake. The challenger, if victorious, inherited the following: the office of the loser, which was to defend a sacred site against any other challenger; the title of lord or king of the country; its revenues, and the person of the loser's wife or daughter. The sacred site could be a forest clearing, a spring or well, an island, or a ford – each, typically, with a single tree (pine or thorn or 'sycamore') which was the scene of the challenge itself. This could be the breaking of a branch from the tree or the blowing of a horn or else the beating of a cymbal hung on the tree. From this are derived several instances of personal combat in which, because there are a number of points of correspondence between the legend and the known facts of prehistory, little doubt is left of pagan antecedents. But the majority of surviving challenge episodes are, not unexpectedly after many centuries of oral transmission, no longer represented by enough diagnostic factors to be reasonably sure that this explanation is correct. Even so, an occasional phrase taken on its own, such as:

> I broke a garland off his tree
> This morning, at the break of day,
> To make him challenge me straight way[34]

may be so exact a fit to the scene at Nemi and so inadequate as a cause of battle without an explanation of this type that it carries conviction of an origin in a ritual act. And although attention has been focused on the examples where a number of elements of the challenge theme are found together, the occurrence of these elements on their own is far from being without interest. The model proposed is likely to be represented after much repetition by a number of eroded and degraded descriptions for every version in which the individual elements have been preserved in an intact group. The elements of the challenge theme are therefore relevant to the assessment of the fit of this model to the observed facts even when they occur in isolation in the 'matter of Britain', as, for example:

Challenges at fountain, ford, glade, island or tomb. Challenges, usually made by a horn or cymbal, involving a tree. Combats in which the winner is obliged to remain and take the place of the loser. Combats in which a successful contender obtains a partner in marriage, particularly if a 'king's daughter' is involved. Personal names, such as the 'Proud One of the Clearing' or the 'Lady of the Fountain' or the 'Knight of the Black Thorn', which are derived from this group of sacred sites.

Water was clearly an important aspect of the religious scene. Apart from 'heads in wells' there is a substantial degree of association between cult sites and water. Hence, in addition to the Lady of the Fountain:

The Lady of the Lake, who brings up the grail-seekers Launcelot and Bohort. The watery ambience of so many challenge situations. The importance of island, lake and fountain in personal names and titles, such as the 'King of the Far Away Isles' or the 'Lady Lile of Avilion'.

The second method of maintaining a virile sacred king on the throne – limiting the period of kingship – may have been superimposed on the first by allowing the challenge to take place only at specific intervals, or it may have involved a periodic election. Candidates seem to have been chosen from visiting strangers who were themselves children of the temple. They might reign for one, seven or fourteen years. The expected type of end-product from this system might be found among the following stories:

Launcelot at the burning city. Launcelot at the waste city. Galahad at the holy city of Sarras. Percival at the Savage Mountain. Bohort at the Castle de la Marche. Gawaine at the island which was defended for seven years. The fay who imposed the 'custom' for seven years. Gawaine and the Green Knight.

In this system the Grail Castle was of prime importance. Its so-called king, we shall find later, was probably a local variant of the lightning god. On this account the victim suffered a blow from a fiery weapon. In the Grail Castle the seeker might find himself in a bed in which he propagated future grail-seekers with a 'daughter' of the 'king', but the bed might prove a 'perilous bed' and when the time came for the seeker's replacement he might be dragged from his consort's arms, mutilated with an axe and then driven through the town in a ritual cart with his feet tied to the shafts and his hands bound behind his back, taunted and pelted with filth. Hence:

The various stories of perilous beds and of the shameful cart.

In the Grail Castle magical barrenness was represented by the Maimed King, to whom sacrifices of a eucharistic nature were made. The blood of the human victim, male or female, was collected in a ritual vessel known as a grail. Hence:

Those aspects of the grail in which it is associated with blood. Other vessels in which blood is collected.

When the sacred king had been chosen, his assumption of office was marked by enthronement in a special seat which, because of the fatal nature of the assignment, was a 'perilous seat' as well as a position of honour. From this type of pagan background probably stem:

Some of the 'perilous' (otherwise known as 'adventurous') seats, palaces, castles or even forests of the 'matter of Britain.' The concept in the *Mabinogion* of a mound with the peculiarity 'that whatever highborn man sits upon it will not go hence without one of two things: wounds or blows, or else his seeing a wonder'.

On his assumption of office, the sacred king adopted clothing or armour of a distinctive colour. Hence:

The 'black knights' who defend fountain and ford and tomb entrance. The black armour used by Owein when he took over guardianship of the fountain from the previous black defender. The red or white knights who defend fountain or ford. The red clothes worn by the beheaded youth at the waste city. The red clothes worn by Galahad when he took his place in the 'siege perilous' at the inception of his grail quest. The way the sitter in the special seat at the Castle de la Marche turned red (translated as 'blushed').

The affairs of sacred kings were a matter of public ceremonial. Hence:

The great plenty of people at the burnt city, with much noise of flutes, bagpipes and viols. The great joy of the crowd. The women who watch with great joy and great pity. The great thronging in the streets of the waste city. The joy of its people. The clerks and priests in long procession praising God. The minstrels who follow the knight in the cart.

The system of belief connected with the grail had a beginning and an end, both of which may be represented in tradition. The arrival of a party of strangers from the east bringing a new cult is perhaps too hackneyed a folk-motif to be relied on as having an origin in reality, but the associated fish meal at the grail table sounds as if it might be a description of a one-time ritual act. The end is equally ill-defined, but the passage which might refer to it will serve as a fitting epilogue to the first section of this book – fitting because although written over a thousand years after the introduction of Christianity, it presents the magical barrenness of the land and the effect on it of a well cult as if they were commonplace realities of everyday life. In doing so, it leaves no doubt about the staying power of these pagan concepts. It also underlines the difficulty of distinguishing between reality and fantasy in the tail-end of a thousand years of oral tradition. The passage is as follows:

The land of Logres became desolate because the wells had failed and the maidens who dwelt in them had vanished. Formerly, travellers could receive at these wells whatever food and drink they wished. A damsel would issue from the well with a gold cup containing meat, pasties and bread. Another would follow, bearing a napkin and a dish of gold and silver with whatever one could desire. [But a stranger and his followers violated the well-maidens and stole their golden cups.] As a result the land became barren; the trees and flowers withered and the waters dried up. No longer could one find the court (le cort) of the Rich Fisher, which used to make the land resplendent with gold and silver, furs, rich stuffs, viands, hawks and falcons. When the court (la cors, la cours) and the Grail were found again, the waters flowed and the fields and trees became green once more.[35]

PART II

The Historical Background
of the
'Arthurian' Sacred Kings

4 Pagan Deities in the Romances

The effect of the foregoing analysis of the 'matter of Britain' is to emphasize the importance of heroes in the pagan cults of that country. A conspicuous feature of this tradition is that individual men and women played out sometimes fatal parts in a vain attempt to promote the well-being of the people at large. But there is more to religion than these priestly surrogates. What of the deities who provide the mainspring, the *raison d'être*, of the whole system? Can they be identified, either by name or style? The names of local deities have been subjected to a long process of verbal transmission, and their attributes are less crisply defined than those of the deities of Greece or Rome; but these matters are by no means beyond conjecture. Welsh legend provides some clues, though the mythological figures in the earliest section of it which are most definitely attested as deities – Lleu, Don, Mabon and Modron – are missing in the 'matter of Britain', or, if they can be detected under garbled versions of their names, play minor (though significantly pagan) roles. However, Welsh tradition enables us to recognize two gods, Bran and Beli, who play major parts in Arthurian stories. These gods, like the gods and goddesses mentioned above, are never actually described as such, but the reasons for thinking them to be so, and their characteristics, would appear as follows to a reader of Welsh legend.

Bran

Bran is not described as a god in Welsh literature; indeed, he is called 'the Blessed' because he is supposed to have introduced Christianity to Britain. There are no inscriptions recording his name in pagan contexts, nor is there any certain Irish parallel. But the suggestion that he is a god, though it relies entirely on inference, rests on good authority. Professor Bromwich says of his portrayal in the *Mabinogion* that it 'forcefully suggests a euhemerized deity' (Loomis 50). Possible correspondences between the literary end-product and the original god are Bran's severed head, which provides abundance and long life for his followers and protection for his country; his great size – no building or boat will hold him; and his cauldron of regeneration. His status as a deity is supported by close association with other pagan figures. He is the son of Llyr, a sea-god common to the British and Irish tradition, about whom little is known. Llyr is the original of Shakespeare's Lear, though in linking Cordelia with him (in which he follows Geoffrey of Monmouth) Shakespeare is probably wrong. Cordelia has a mythological original in Creiddylad, daughter of the Welsh god Lludd (also a sea-god), of whom it is said that two mythological figures, Gwyn and Gwythyr, are to do battle for her each May 1st until doomsday, when the victor shall have the maiden.[36]

The way in which Bran died, by a wound in the foot from a poisoned spear, suggests, according to Bromwich, 'comparison with the Fisher King's wound through the thighs' (Loomis 51). His title 'Blessed', far from having a Christian origin, is probably a corruption of some earlier epithet which began with the Welsh word for head – Bran's severed head being his most prominent feature in the underlying mythology.

Beli

Beli, or as he is sometimes known, Beli Mawr (Beli the Great), is not mentioned in inscriptions nor has he an Irish parallel recognizable as a deity. Like Bran, his status as a god – 'the common ancestor deity of the leading Welsh dynasties'[37] – depends on inference. And, unfortunately, no actions or attributes are recorded in Welsh tradition which might give a lead to cult practice or dogma. There is only one clue, provided by the Irish Celticist T. F. O'Rahilly, who suggests that Beli's name is related to the Irish word for lightning – a most suitable characteristic for a god.

Beli's original importance may have been greater than the paucity of information about him implies. Welsh tradition has it that his name is used in one of the earliest surviving names by which Britain was known to its inhabitants. This was Ynys Veli, which might be either the Island of Beli or the Island of Meli (Honey). Since neighbouring islands, Ireland

and Man, owe their names to mythological personages, the first of these alternatives is probably to be preferred.

Bran in the 'matter of Britain'

When we turn from Welsh legend to the 'matter of Britain', we find Bran in various garbled forms and compound names. The field has been comprehensively reviewed by Helaine Newstead in *Bran the Blessed in Arthurian Romance*. She speaks entirely from the literary point of view, and without any emphasis on the mythological aspects of her subject, but her lines of reasoning are valid for our present purpose. She makes it clear that the following characters are derived from the Welsh Bran or closely related to him by their behaviour: Brangor, Bran de Lis, Brangemeur, Brandus des Illes, Bron, Brennius, Brien, Ban, Bandemagus (or Baudemagus), the Fisher Kings, Anfortas, the Grail King in *Diu Crône*, Evrain (King of Brandigan), and a number of unnamed knights and kings. Some of these are recognizable because of their names, others because they possess several of the characteristic features of the group. Taken together, these features add up to the most complete picture of a native deity that has so far been obtained. According to Newstead's analysis, Bran is most consistently associated with abundance; he is wounded or languishing; he is connected with islands or water; he is a giant, or, if represented as a mere human being, of more than human stature; he is connected with severed heads, corpses and the drinking of blood; and his companions are untouched by age. Although not so intended by Newstead, this list is a compendium of paganism.

In her review of about thirty characters and situations from the 'matter of Britain', roughly half of which are identified by names resembling Bran, Newstead has followed up a group of features primarily linked with a Welsh figure. She has demonstrated the extraordinary degree of penetration of this traditional personage, who is in fact a pagan deity, into the French romances. This is a matter of considerable importance to those interested in the origins of the Arthurian Cycle, but little new about paganism has been revealed. As far as the main outlines of the picture are concerned, Newstead's Bran is very much the same as the Bran of the *Mabinogion*. It is only when we examine the detail that we realize how substantially study of the 'matter of Britain' has increased our knowledge of this deity. Take, for instance, the affairs at the Grail Castle. Here Bran both provides the background and has an interest in the cast – as Fisher King he is a Grail-keeper, and as Ban he is the ancestor of grail-seekers. Again, Bran (as Brangoire) owns the 'castle' where Bors wins the princess in the anniversary tournament. And, as far as the head cult is concerned, Bran (as Ban) is the father of Launcelot who cut off the head for Meleagant's sister to throw into the well, and he is also (as Baudemagus) the father or stepfather of this girl. In addition to all this, the nature of the debilitating wound between the thighs, castration, is made explicit in the case of Anfortas, who is considered by Newstead to be an equivalent of Bran. Clearly Bran has a special relationship to the sacred kings of earlier chapters, and is one of the deities in whose names they took on their temporary divine status.

Beli in the 'matter of Britain'

The only clue to the identification of Beli in the romances lies in the significance of his name (details are given on p. 118). The sword which bears a variant of Beli's name is used in a ritual act in the same way as Balin's sword, which suggests that Beli and Balin are the same. Certainly Balin has an appropriately wide range of pagan characteristics to fit the suggestion that he owes his origin to a god. Balin, however, is only one of several possible end-products of the recollection in tradition of this particular deity. Loomis considered that Pelles (the lord of the Grail Castle) derives from the Welsh Beli, and it has been suggested that Pellinore is a distortion of Beli Mawr – the change from 'B' to 'P' at a Welsh/English interface being a common enough occurrence. At first glance, there might seem to be a substantial contradiction in these three attributions taken together. Balin and Pelles seem poles apart, one the epitome of action and adventure whereas the other is the static lord of a castle he does not leave after he has been maimed. There is a good deal of overlap in the characteristics of Pellinore and Pelles. Both are maimed kings (Sommer VII 243, Malory XVII 5); both have daughters who play significant parts in the quest for the grail; and Pellinore's son and Pelles's grandson are both successful in the quest. But Balin, in contrast, fights the defender of an island, strikes the Dolorous Stroke and in general leads a vigorous life. Yet if these activities are examined more closely it will be apparent that they are all part of the same system of paganism. Balin fights a knight who meets all comers on an island; Pellinore takes on all comers at a fountain (Malory I 23); Balin strikes the Dolorous Stroke; Pelles's grandson heals the recipient; Balin's companion bleeds a dish of blood, so does Pellinore's daughter; Balin wields the lightning sword; the spear which wounds Pellinore between the thighs comes like lightning from the sky (Sommer VII 243).

The pagan associations of all three thus overlap to a considerable extent. Any appearance of contradiction is because the active aspects of the system, appropriate to the human representative of the deity, have coalesced round Balin and, to a certain extent, round Pellinore. But this should not be taken to mean that Balin has a different origin. It is not illogical to suppose that the name of the deity has clung to the wielder of the lightning sword and the recipient of the blow. We are merely seeing two sides of the same coin.

The name under discussion may occur in cult contexts in two geographical locations. Barenton, the hill and cult well in that prime Arthurian locality in Brittany, the forest of Broceliande, was originally Belenton – perhaps a contraction from Beli Nemeton. And Tombelaine, associated in folk-tale with Mont St Michel, could also embody a recollection of this deity.[38]

Personal names from the oral tradition are subject to considerable distortion, and some variants get separated from their contexts so that they can no longer be equated with the main forms with certainty. There are a number of such variants of Balin in the 'matter of Britain', and there is a particularly interesting possible variant of Beli in Welsh tradition. W. A. Nitze considered the possibility that Pwyll, as well as Pelles and Beli and Bilis (another form of Beli in the 'matter of Britain') might originally have been the same person (Loomis 267). Since Pwyll was prince of Dyfed in south-west Wales, to equate Pwyll with Beli, and hence with Balin, would carry the associations of a cult we shall find linked with a floated stone to the source of the bluestones themselves.

Bran and Beli are linked together by tradition in several ways. Bran is Beli's grandson in the *Mabinogion*, but in other sources the two are often paired, generally as brothers. Possible instances are Bran and his brother, the dwarf king Beli, in *Erec*; Geoffrey of Monmouth's Brennius and his brother Belinus,[39] who shared the crown of Britain; Balan (who C. Squire suggests to be a form of Bran[40]) and his brother Balin; and the gods Brennos and Bolgios who led their peoples into Macedonia in the third century BC.

Goddesses, of course, feature as well as gods, and since the first two to be considered are given their proper descriptions in the 'matter of Britain', there is no need to look for initial clues in Celtic language sources.

Morgan le Fay

The personage most frequently referred to as a deity in the 'matter of Britain' and associated material is Morgan le Fay. Quite apart from her title 'le Fay', which implies a connection with the supernatural, she is referred to as 'Morgne the goddes' in *Gawain and the Green Knight*; as 'Dea' (but qualified by the word 'imaginary') by Giraldus Cambrensis; and as 'Deess' in French versions. It is unlikely that the idea of Morgan as a goddess was invented during the Middle Ages. The probability is that she had her origin as a pagan deity. One of the most clearly marked associations between Morgan and paganism is apparent in the earliest literary reference to her. She is described by Geoffrey of Monmouth as 'the fairest and chief of nine enchantresses skilled in flying through the air and in the art of healing. They dwell on an island of amazing fertility', which Loomis suggests we can easily recognize as the Isle of Avalon, for 'hither Arthur was brought after the battle of Camblan'.[41] Nine priestesses on an island is attested as an aspect of paganism by Pomponius Mela, who in the first century AD described the cult which existed in his day on the island of Sena – the modern Sein, lying off a narrow, westward-pointing Breton peninsula (the Point du Raz), a tiny, windswept island which is said to have remained pagan almost until modern times. Here there were nine oracular priestesses, dedicated to virginity, who were reputed to control the winds and the waves, to transform themselves into animal shape, to heal and to predict the future. The same motif, nine maidens who tend an oracle on an 'otherworld' island, is to be found in an early Welsh poem, 'The Spoils of Annwm':

> My first utterance, it is from the cauldron that it was spoken.
> By the breath of nine maidens it [i.e. the cauldron] was kindled.[42]

The location of this cauldron of inspiration was apparently on an island off the coast of Wales, perhaps Grassholm, which, lying some miles off a westward-pointing peninsula, has a remarkable resemblance in its situation to Sein. It is difficult to believe that the same pattern should be repeated in three entirely different circumstances without some underlying reality. It is possible that there may historically have been nine priestesses on these and perhaps other islands. Or an image may have emerged from the coalescence in a literary setting of individual factors from pagan thought-patterns – westerly situations, islands, priestesses, the number nine, the relationship of religion to natural phenomena. Either way, there is a strong association between Morgan the Goddess and several major elements of paganism.

Morgan has sometimes been equated with those major figures from the pagan world, the Welsh Modron and the Irish Morrigan, but 'equation' implies a greater identity than the surviving legends indicate. Yet it cannot be considered irrelevant that these three should share a number of characteristics which can reasonably be considered as residues of paganism. In so far as these characteristics belong to Morgan, her position as a deity is reinforced by still more links with the supernatural. For instance, she appears as one of a trio of fays in several romances.[43] Triple form is an aspect of the Morrigan and is common in representations of the Mother Goddess. Again, Morgan appears as either a hag or a beautiful young woman, or as either a protector or a destroyer, as do Irish goddesses. According to Loomis,[44] Morgan was the nameless fay who intervened in a battle at a ford in the shape of a black bird; the Morrigan also took part in a battle at a ford and left the scene in the form of a crow.[45] In addition, Morgan and Modron are both described as the mother of Owein;[46] an unnamed parallel of Morgan, who lived in an island paradise,[47] and Modron are both identified as the mother of the god Mabon; and both the mother of Owein and the Morrigan are washers at fords who conceive as a result of intercourse at the ford. Another resemblance between Morgan and Modron is that the former is said to be the daughter of Avallo or Avalloc, and the latter of Avallach, names in one way or another closely associated with that otherworld of healing and plenty which finds its best-known expression in Malory's Vale of Avilion.

Morgan thus appears to have a substantial association with the factors which enter into the make-up of a pagan goddess: intercourse leading to the conception of a hero; a strong connection with water; metamorphosis into bird or animal form; magical control over natural phenomena; healing; and membership of the royal house of an otherworld island of all delights.

Diana of the Wood and Dyonas

Another deity specifically mentioned in the 'matter of Britain' is Diane, goddess of the wood (Sommer II 208), the mother of Dyonas, who is the father of Vivienne (or Nimue or Elaine), the 'Damsel of the Lake'. How the name of the Roman goddess worshipped at Nemi should have cropped up in a medieval French story is a puzzle. Perhaps the Romans brought the cult of Diana of the Wood, and the name was remembered as the equivalent of a local deity, or alternatively the name may have been used by a learned editor of traditional tales to describe a remnant of paganism in terms intelligible to his readers. But aside from the name, the goddess of the grove at Nemi fits easily into the local scene with its multitude of personal combats at fountain, glade and ford. And perhaps we can conclude from the close relationship between Diane, goddess of the wood, and the 'Damsel of the Lake' that this native nymph plays a part in the local cult as important as that of Egeria in the Classical example. But what of the intervening Dyonas? This is a name which, in the context of the worship of Diana, would readily have been understood in Classical times as being the equivalent of Dianus or Janus. Frazer explains the relationship after putting forward his conclusion that

at Nemi the King of the Wood personated the oak-god Jupiter and mated with the oak-goddess Diana in the sacred grove. An echo of their mystic union has come down to us in the legend of the loves of Numa and Egeria, who according to some had their trysting place in these holy woods.

79

To this theory it may naturally be objected that the divine consort of Jupiter was not Diana but Juno, and that if Diana had a mate at all he might be expected to bear the name not of Jupiter, but of Dianus or Janus, the latter of these forms being merely a corruption of the former. All this is true, but the objection may be parried by observing that the two pairs of deities, Jupiter and Juno on the one side, and Dianus and Diana, or Janus and Jana, on the other side, are merely duplicates of each other, their names and their functions being in substance and origin identical. With regard to their names, all four of them come from the same Aryan root *DI*, meaning 'bright', which occurs in the names of the corresponding Greek deities, Zeus and his old female consort Dione.[48]

Dyonas, therefore, in spite of having slipped a generation relative to the Classical example, is to be understood as being a local variant on the widespread motif of the god of thunder and lightning. The close relationship of this local Zeus to a native water nymph in tradition is matched in material remains by a dedication at the hot spring at Bath to Lightning in company with the goddess of the sacred grove, Nemetona,[49] (Nemi again).

Another mention of a Classical god in an early non-Welsh source occurs in the description by Geoffrey of Monmouth of the burial of King Lear in a certain underground chamber which Cordelia 'had bidden be made under the river Soar at Leicester. This underground chamber was founded in honour of the two-faced Janus, and there, when the yearly celebration of the day came round, did all the workmen of the city set hand unto such work as they were about to be busied upon throughout the year.'[50] Here the name Janus crops up again, and so do those typical pagan motifs, the year-end celebration and a river. The two-faced Janus is reminiscent of the two-faced representations of human heads which, along with the more common three-faced heads, are typical material recollections of the head cult. Besides this reference to Janus, Geoffrey of Monmouth speaks of a prophesy by Merlin to the heathen Vortigern of a time to come after which Janus shall never have priests again. However imaginative Geoffrey may have been, he did not people his pages with pagan deities. It is therefore reasonable to suggest that these two mentions of the god Janus reinforce the explanation of the reference to Dyonas as being a relic of paganism, whether on account of the retention of the name from the depths of an Indo-European past or a similarity of cult to the classical deity of the same name.

As well as these specific references to deities in the 'matter of Britain', there are numerous hints of paganism which in one or two instances are sufficiently repetitive to suggest the form of a deity who has not yet been described as such in these pages. For instance, the Dame of the Lake and her damsels may be thought to have overlapping aspects of goddess and nymph. In this connection a name occurs which has attracted little attention as a possible goddess by commentators on British paganism. This is Elaine (or Elayne, Eleyne, Helayne or simply Helen or Elen). As wife of King Ban (a form of Bran), an Elaine is the mother of the hero Launcelot; as the daughter of Pelles (a maimed king), an Elaine is the mother of the hero Galahad; as the daughter of 'the Lady of the Rule' by Pellinore (a maimed king), an Elayne had the Warrior of the Glade for her lover and her severed head was found by a well; as daughter of King Howell, a Helena is connected with Mont St Michel (which is very likely to have been a cult site)*; yet another Elaine is the sister of the goddess Morgan le Fay; and since Elaine is one of the names of the Lady of the Lake, her underwater abode and her ride in the 'demeaning' cart add to the suggestion of pagan origin. All these associations with cult figures and cult activities from the 'matter of Britain' reinforce the supposition which might be made from Helen's preeminence in Welsh tradition that she was a goddess, but it is unusual to see a clear statement to this effect as in D. D. R. Owen's *The Evolution of the Grail Legend*.[51]

Of the deities mentioned in this chapter, most information from traditional sources concerns Bran. This emphasis might merely be the accident of survival but it might equally represent the importance of Bran in the underlying tradition. If so, it matches the predominance of the head cult in late Celtic times, noted by Ross.[52]

---

*The Saint Michael's Mounts – Mont St Michel, St Michael's Mount in Cornwall, Skellig Michael, and Glastonbury Tor, with its chapel of St Michael on top – presumably owe their names to Christian response to their original cult use. It can scarcely be an accident that these pinnacles of rock surrounded by water should all have required the forceful presence of the principal militant champion of Christianity.

5 Time-scale

The picture of native paganism presented by tradition is inevitably of the latest phase. Classical descriptions may take us somewhat further back, but to no more than a century or so BC (with one or two exceptions). Prior to that, archaeology must hold the field, and our chances of linking the ephemeral matter of the spoken word to the material substratum appear neglible. This is a great pity. The affairs of the house of Atreus lend Mycenae an extra dimension, which is completely missing at, say, Avebury.

Written dedications dating from the Roman occupation give a smattering of names of native deities from the period before the invasion, and by linking them with members of the official Roman pantheon give an indication of the type of cult associated with them. Ross, for example, lists nearly twenty names of British warrior gods which have been preserved in this way and linked with Mars. But earlier than that, British prehistoric remains are completely lacking in reliable associations with the names of gods or men. Even the nature of the cults practised at well-known sites is a matter of guesswork and is limited to the most basic concepts of primitive religion. There is a general presumption that the mother-goddess was pre-eminent throughout prehistory; that the cereal growers of Neolithic times (and perhaps later) would have observed annual ceremonies which evoked the death and rebirth of the year; and that in the Bronze Age, with its increasing Indo-European content, power swung to male-dominated pantheons. But that is about all. The presence of elaborate burial arrangements, of cult sites and of sacrificial deposits shows intense religious feeling, but there is an impersonal air about them because we do not know, for the most part, what deity was worshipped nor why. The most interesting exceptions are those cases where an incised symbol can be interpreted. This occurs at Stonehenge, where as well as the carved axes there is a reliably identified representation of the mother-goddess, but even these give no indication of ritual or dogma. Our only hope of shedding light on this area is by reference to outside comment from literate Classical sources or to native tradition.

Although the Greeks were familiar with the island's name, the most complete description from early times of an island which might be Britain gives no name but calls the inhabitants 'Hyperboreans' – dwellers beyond the north wind – a fanciful term for which no specific locality can be determined. However, since the description refers to an island in the ocean, not smaller than Sicily, lying to the North, opposite the coast of Celtic Gaul, it will have to be scrutinized carefully to see if internal evidence supports the obvious conclusion that Britain is intended. The report is from not later than the fourth century B C, relayed by Diodorus Siculus, who lived in the first century B C, from a lost work of Hecateus:

This island is of a happy temperature, rich in soil and fruitful in everything, yielding its produce twice in the year. Tradition says that Latona was born there, and for that reason the inhabitants venerate Apollo more than any other god. They are, in a manner, his priests, for they daily celebrate him with continual songs of praise and pay him abundant honours.

In this island, there is a magnificent grove (or precinct) of Apollo, and a remarkable temple, of a round form, adorned with many consecrated gifts. There is also a city, sacred to the same God, most of the inhabitants of which are harpers, who continually play upon their harps in the temple, and sing hymns to the God, extolling his actions. The Hyperboreans use a peculiar dialect, and have a remarkable attachment to the Greeks, especially to the Athenians and the Delians, deducing their friendship from remote periods. It is related that some Greeks formerly visited the Hyperboreans, with whom they left consecrated gifts of great value, and also that in ancient times Abaris, coming from the Hyperboreans into Greece, renewed their family intercourse with the Delians.

It is also said that on this island the moon appears very near to the earth, that certain eminences of a terrestrial form are plainly seen in it, that Apollo visits the island once in a course of nineteen years, in which period the stars complete their revolutions, and that for this reason the Greeks distinguish the cycle of nineteen years by the name of 'the great year'. During the season of his appearance the God plays upon the harp and dances every night, from the vernal equinox until the rising of the Pleiads, pleased with his own successes. The supreme authority in that city and the sacred precinct is vested in those who are called Boreadae, being the descendants of Boreas, and their governments have been uninterruptedly transmitted in this line.[53]

83

Clearly this report is of great importance to the study of native paganism if it refers to Britain. But does it? Any analysis of this ancient record may as well begin, as Diodorus did, with the location of the island. If, in spite of the 'Hyperboreans', we are talking of a real geographical situation, then the size and position exclude by a substantial margin any islands other than Britain, Ireland and the improbable Iceland.

Then there is the round form of the temple. Circular shape in western prehistoric monuments is characteristic of, and more or less confined to, the British province (including Brittany and Ireland). One of the more conspicuous circular constructions, probably in the south of Britain, may have been reported to the Greeks. Stonehenge, in particular, was still in use and, over 1000 years after its completion, unique in Europe for its architectural use of massive dressed stones. The reference to Apollo, quoted by Diodorus, would favour an identification with Stonehenge because this structure is aligned to the sun, of which Apollo was the deity.

These points of correspondence between the Classical report and the likely state of Britain in the period referred to have been known for some time. More recently, another similarity has been noticed. The report suggests that the moon was of great interest at that time. The 'eminences of terrestrial form' on the moon bespeak close observation and so does the reference to the nineteen year cycle after which the phases of the moon repeat themselves on the same calendar dates. This interest in the moon matches the current view that some Megalithic settings of standing stones might have been oriented towards points on the moon's cycle of movement along the horizon.

There seems to be a fairly good chance that Hecateus's account refers to Britain and that the circular temple is Stonehenge. The objects of veneration there – the sun and the moon – were still those which had decided the placing of the stones so many centuries before, and archaeology confirms that the site continued in use until after the time of Hecateus.

When the Classical account refers to Apollo, the Greek name reveals an aspect of the cult, but it conceals the native name of the deity. A later inscription gives more information about 'Apollo' in Britain. He is equated with Maponius, the Mabon of Welsh tradition, a name which appears in compound form as the Mabonagrain of the romances. Mabon implies 'son', and is regularly associated with his mother in the phrase Mabon son of Modron, in which Modron means 'mother'. 'Son, son of Mother' may be taken to imply the 'Divine Youth, son of the Divine Mother' in this context of deities. And since the Classical account refers to Apollo in conjunction with his mother, Latona, it is possible that the native original was some 'son and mother' pair. Once again we are thinking in terms of an aspect of a cult rather than a name. Modron's named son is Owein, the typical challenge-knight, and since Mabonagrain is to be found in *Erec* defending a site with a sycamore, it is not unreasonable to suggest that a cult of this type was associated with the British 'Apollo'.

Other parts of the description of the activities at the city and the temple – the 'grove', music and song, and ceremonial gifts – lend verisimilitude to the scene. And since human beings may play the part of deities, even the dancing and harp-playing of the god may once have been a visible and audible representation of his presence.

It might be thought that no native tradition could possibly be older than this Classical description of Early Iron Age Britain, yet by a remarkable chance the recollection of a single memorable event from the Early Bronze Age survived in the oral tradition and was incorporated in a written work of the twelfth century. This most intriguing survival (briefly mentioned in the introduction) is of the moving of the bluestones of the earliest above-ground construction at Stone-henge from south-west Wales to Salisbury Plain, and it is to be found in that most unreliable of sources, the *Historia* of Geoffrey of Monmouth. This author failed to put the episode in its correct historical sequence. It is mixed up with the period immediately following the end of the Roman occupation, and is cast in the mould of magic and superstition. Nevertheless, the account is recognizable as an attenuated memory of the past because it states that the stones were moved from a distance and that they were carried by water. The former has been known to be the case since 1923, when H. H. Thomas[54] showed that the bluestones were of several types of rock found in the Prescelly Mountains in Pembroke-shire; and it is generally considered that the stones were carried for the greater part of their journey by sea. It cannot be argued that Geoffrey was making an intelligent guess. Lack of knowledge of geology in the Middle Ages would have prevented his attributing distant origin from the type of rock. Indeed, no such thought occurred even in the enlightened eighteenth century. It was not until the nineteenth that it was realized that the bluestones were not of local provenance, and not until the twentieth that their distant origin, with its intervening sea-journey, was recognized. The possibility that there is a correspondence between a tradition of the twelfth century and an event which occurred more than (perhaps considerably more than[55]) 3000 years before, and the possibility that we have a verbal description, however distorted, of an event so early in our history, are both so interesting that we must give Geoffrey's account careful consideration.

What Geoffrey of Monmouth said is roughly as follows: After the departure of the Romans, Britain was left undefended. A British ruler called Vortigern came to an arrangement with Saxon mercenaries but failed to dislodge them when they became colonists. He was replaced by Aurelius Ambrosius, who rallied the native British and achieved some success against the Saxons. Having triumphed over his enemies, Aurelius Ambrosius wished to commemorate some of his countrymen, who had been treacherously slain by the Saxons, with a lasting memorial. He was advised to consult Vortigern's prophet, Merlin, who was requested to come to the king from the Fountain of Galabes (in the land of the Gewissae), which Merlin was 'wont to haunt'. Merlin said:

If thou be fain to grace the burial-place of these men with a work that shall endure for ever, send for the Dance of the Giants that is in Killare, a mountain in Ireland. For a structure of stones is there that none of this age could arise save his wit were strong enough to carry his art. For the stones be big, nor is there stone anywhere of more virtue, and, so they be set up round this plot in a circle, even as they be now there set up, here they shall stand for ever. . . . [The king, Aurelius Ambrosius, was sceptical about the value of the stones but Merlin claimed that in the stones were] a mystery and a healing virtue against many ailments. Giants of old did carry them from the furthest ends of Africa and did set them up in Ireland what time they did inhabit therein. . . . [Convinced by these arguments, the king sent off his brother, Uther Pendragon, and Merlin with a force of armed men to collect the stones. Their landing in Ireland was opposed by Gilloman, the young king of Ireland, but the Britons prevailed and pressed] forward to Mount Killare, and when they reached the structure of stones rejoiced and marvelled greatly. . . . [Merlin put together his own engines and] at last, when he had set in place everything whatsoever that was needed, he laid down the stones so lightly as none would believe, and when he had laid them down, bade carry them to the ships and place them inboard, and on this wise did they again set sail and returned unto Britain with joy, presently with a fair wind making land, and fetching the stones to the burial place ready to set up . . . [After Aurelius Ambrosius had crowned himself at Whitsuntide at the Mount of Amesbury (according to E. Ekwall,[56] Ambr's Burg), he] bade Merlin set up the stones that he had brought from Ireland around the burial-place. Merlin accordingly obeyed his ordinance, and set up the stones about the compass of the burial-ground in such wise as they had stood upon Mount Killare in Ireland, and proved yet once again how skill surpasseth strength.

Later, the son of Vortigern revolted against Aurelius Ambrosius and, making common cause with Gilloman, issued forth from St David's against Uther Pendragon. Both the king of Ireland and the son of Vortigern were killed about half a day's march from St David's, which is about twenty miles from the Prescelly Mountains. Aurelius Ambrosius died about this time and was buried within the Giants' Dance. Uther Pendragon was then crowned king, later to be followed by his son Arthur.

This is not the only instance of stones being erected by Merlin, and the others must be described before an analysis is attempted. But two points call for an immediate explanation. The first is the reference to Ireland instead of south-west Wales. This is sometimes thought of as an exaggeration. The stones came from far to the west by sea, so within the limits of accuracy of the oral tradition this may seem a pardonable divergence from the truth. But a better explanation is that some Irish influence extended to Pembrokeshire, or else that the word which today has the connotation 'Ireland' had a wider distribution in those remote times and probably a religious significance. The latter explanation fits Geoffrey of Monmouth's reference to the killing of the king of Ireland near to the source of the bluestones. And it can be said that the name 'Ireland' often occurs in association with cult activities – a challenge knight is a brother (or son) of the queen of Ireland; Bran's sister, Branwen, married the king of Ireland; and Pelles was riding 'towards Ireland' (Malory XVII 5) when he came to the ship in which he was smitten through the thighs.

The second matter calling for an immediate explanation is the unexpected length of the survival of the tradition. If it were not for this sole instance, a span of 3000 years from the originating circumstance to the earliest surviving written version would be thought impossible. Professor Piggott's opinion that this episode is a relic of Bronze Age oral 'literature' has already been quoted, and so has the suggestion that the most probable means of transmission was the priestly chants of a continuing community. More recently, archaeologists have placed great emphasis on continuity of culture in Britain, particularly from the time of the bluestone move to the threshold of the Roman occupation. It is thus not unreasonable to suppose that a recollection of Bronze Age native paganism survived late enough to be written down.

6 Camelot and Sarras

It is not uncommon to find, in traditional material, more than one version of an episode. L. V. Grinsell mentions several variants of the Giants' Dance[57] but they are relatively recent and carry no new information about the original circumstances of the removal. However, there are other, much earlier, potential variants on the theme of the Giants' Dance – incidents in which Merlin erects or even floats stones – which have so far escaped attention. The reason for this neglect is that the alternative forms are in the romances; but since the 'matter of Britain' has been shown to have many points of contact with tradition, it will be worth examining these stone-moving episodes to see if their associations link them with Geoffrey of Monmouth's story. They are as follows.

The Peron

. . . the peron that Merlin had made to-fore, where Sir Lanceor, that was king's son of Ireland, was slain by the hands of Balin (Malory X 5)

When Arthur, at the beginning of his reign, was menaced by the rebellion of eleven kings, headed by King Rience of North Wales, he called a council-general at Camelot. After all Arthur's knights had assembled, a damsel sent by the Lady Lile of Avilion brought in a sword which was offered to a knight surpassing in skill and uprightness, who would be able to draw the sword from its scabbard without the use of force. All failed in the attempt except Balin, a poor knight of Northumberland. At this moment, the Lady of the Lake came into the court and demanded from Arthur the head of the knight who had won the sword, or else the head of the damsel that had brought it. When Balin was told this, he cut off the head of the Lady of the Lake, took it up, and rode out of the town. Lanceor then requested Arthur's leave to 'revenge the despite' that Balin had done. He caught up with him in a little space and challenged him, but Lanceor perished in the ensuing battle. A damsel called Colombe then rode up and, grieving for the dead Lanceor, slew herself. Balin left the scene of the double tragedy and rode on to meet his brother Balan. Together they captured King Rience and sent him captive to King Arthur. Later they played a predominant part in the defeat of the remaining rebel kings. Meanwhile King Mark of Cornwall came upon the dead lovers by chance, searched for a tomb for them, and had them buried. Merlin, although he plays no active part, is a constant presence at these events, explaining the relationship of the participants, prophesying misfortune to the successful drawer of the sword, prophesying later events at the place of combat, prophesying that Balin would strike the Dolorous Stroke, and assisting Balin and Balan in their campaign against Rience and the eleven kings.

That the peron (a block of stone used as a platform) was at the place of combat is made clear by references to it, much later in the story, as a meeting-place. Apart from the quotation at the head of this section, these are 'where Merlin set the peron' (Malory X 2), 'the stony grave that Merlin set beside Camelot' (X 16), and 'the peron and the grave beside Camelot' (X 87). They have nothing to add to the earlier description of the events at the site except that the interment of Lanceor and Colombe 'under one stone' is credited to the 'craft of Merlin'.

The Floating Stone

. . . the stone hoving on the water (Malory XIII 5)

After the defeat of the rebel kings, Balin encountered a series of adventures. This included an incident in which a 'damosel bled for the custom of a castle' so that the lady of the castle should be healed (Malory II 13), and, in another castle, the striking by Balin of the Dolorous Stroke against King Pellam, on account of which three countries were destroyed. Eventually Balin came to a castle where he was met by the blast of a horn, which he significantly recognized as 'blown for me, for I am the prize and yet I am not dead' (Malory II 17). There was 'dancing and minstrelsy and all manner of joy', but, as the chief lady of the castle explained, the custom was that he must 'joust with a knight hereby that keepeth an island'. The defending knight, who was dressed in red, was, unknown to Balin, his brother Balan. The two fought until both were mortally wounded before recognizing each other, when Balan, lamenting their unhappy state, remarked that he had been unable to leave the island since he came there, 'for here it happed me to slay a knight that kept this island, and since might I never depart, and no more should ye, brother, an ye might have slain me as ye have, and escaped yourself with the life' (II 18). Merlin 'buried them both in one tomb' (II 19) and, after sundry miraculous actions, 'let make by his subtilty that Balin's sword was put in a marble stone standing upright as great as a mill stone, and the stone hoved always above the water and did many years, and so by adventure it swam down the stream to the City of Camelot . . .' (II 19). The stone reached Camelot on a certain feast of Pentecost, when King Arthur and the company assembled at his court were awaiting some 'adventure'. At this moment, Galahad, dressed in red, was introduced to the court and took his place in the 'siege perilous'. He drew the sword from the stone, signalling the beginning of 'the adventures of the Sangreal' (XIII 2) and of the process that led to his own year-end death at the holy city of Sarras.

The events recounted here are of great importance in the editorial organization of *Morte Darthur*. Malory uses several of them to link the early part of the book, in which Arthur consolidates his position, with later stages. Thus he looks forward from the Dolorous Stroke to the ultimate healing of the Maimed King on the Grail Quest; from the dish of blood in this story to the dish bled by Percival's sister on her fatal journey to Sarras; and from the prophesy of injury to Gawaine when he unsuccessfully tried to draw the sword from the floated stone, to the sad finale.

For us, these events have a different significance. Apart from those salient features of Balin's 'life' that have already been used to suggest that he corresponds to the god Beli, there is a wealth of allusion here to personages and events of pagan ambience. We see that Malory's editorial process is no more than an emphasis on the fundamental pagan structure of the 'matter of Britain', and that the pagan scene in which the 'peron' and the 'floating stone' are set both ties them together and links them with the scheme of sacred kingship

TABLE I

Reality	The		floated and erected	stones	of Stonehenge originally came from the
Source	1	2	3		4
A Geoffrey of Monmouth	MERLIN, who	floated and erected	STONES	taken by force from	'IRELAND' (whose
B Malory X 5	MERLIN	set up a		STONE	where the son of 'IRELAND'S'
C Malory II 19	MERLIN	floated a		STONE	in which he had set

already elaborated. What now remains is to show the relationship of these two episodes to the moving and erection of the Giants' Dance.

To do this it will be convenient first to isolate the relevant factors on which a comparison can be based. In 'the peron' they are: Merlin erected a stone monument where the king of Ireland's son was killed by Balin. In 'the floating stone': Merlin floated a stone, from which Galahad later withdrew Balin's sword and in doing so inaugurated the grail quest.

Next we must examine the cult background to the Giants' Dance episode itself. The possibility that Geoffrey's supporting detail could be significant seems never to have been explored. Yet the presence of a fountain is at once suggestive of a cult activity, particularly as standing stones are known to be associated with sacred waters. F. Jones, in *Holy Wells of Wales*, notes no fewer than seventeen examples in Pembrokeshire, which is more than three times the average number for Welsh counties. The name of the spring provides further information, for Galabes, in the forms Galaphes and Kalafes, is a name found in the 'matter of Britain'. (There is not always a clear-cut distinction in the oral tradition between 'b' and 'v' or 'f'.) Galaphes, we are told (Sommer I 289), was wounded by a fiery man in the castle of Corbenic which he lly Mountains.

| 5 | 6 |

as later killed near the Prescelly Mts), frequented a fountain associated with a GRAIL HERO.

was killed at the hands of BALIN

BALIN's sword. The sword and stone were associated with a GRAIL HERO.

had himself built to hold the grail. Comparison of this incident with others of a similar nature leads to the conclusion that Galaphes was involved in a lightning cult. This would be appropriate to the circumstances of Stonehenge at the time of the bluestone move because the change at that time to an open sun-oriented form of temple might represent the arrival of a sky-god. As J. and C. H. Hawkes say,[58] 'it was the strong Indo-European element infused into our Beaker culture by the Battle-Axe warriors which gave its religion this skyward trend. We are witnessing the triumph of some more barbaric Zeus over the ancient Earth mother dear to the Neolithic peasantry. . . .' And later in the Stonehenge sequence there are the incised axes which, since the axe is sometimes used as a symbol for lightning in representations of the thunder-god, could be taken as having the same implication.

To set against this, there are references to Balin in the other accounts of stones moved by Merlin, and in one of them to Balin's sword. As Balin may be taken to be a lightning-god, and his sword a representation of the lightning, there is a correspondence here with the same type of cult in the background to the Giants' Dance. There is a second correspondence in the death of a member of the royal house of 'Ireland' in one of these alternative accounts, and there is a third in the association with the grail cult in the other. The relevant factors are set out in tabular form for easier comparison. They are as follows:

1 Merlin
2 floated or erected
3 a stone or stones
4 Ireland's king or prince killed
5 an association with Balin
6 an association with a grail hero

The relationship of these motifs in the episodes under consideration is shown in Table 1.

The relationship between the three episodes as we see it at this stage in the analysis can be shown more clearly by looking at the pattern in which the motifs occur. It is as follows:

TABLE 2

A	1	2	3	4		6	The Giants' Dance
B	1	2	3	4	5		The Peron
C	1	2	3		5	6	The Floating Stone

This is the sort of pattern of survival which would be expected from the erosion during oral transmission of stories which had a common origin containing all six motifs.

The chance that we will be right in supposing that the common factors of these three episodes indicate a common origin is much greater than the mathematical odds against this number of correspondences being mere coincidence, for two reasons. One is that the tenor of all three is religious. This can be seen by the presence of Balin and the Grail cult among the motifs, and the various pagan elements in the background of B and C. Although the latter is not matched in A, we must expect religion to have bulked large in the tales told by succeeding generations about this unique act of removal. The other is the specific nature of one of the pagan motifs, the association with Balin, and especially the nature of 'Balin's sword', fixed by Merlin in the floating stone. Its lightning symbolism is, as mentioned above, particularly suited to the circumstances of Stonehenge at the time of the moving of the bluestones.

This analysis of the stories of stones erected or floated by Merlin shows that there are two sorts of correspondence. One is between the episodes themselves, which contain common terms. The other is between the stone-moving episodes as a group and the picture of paganism so far built up in this book.

The direction in which this enquiry is moving is towards the proposition that tradition has preserved some sort of recollection of social behaviour at the beginning of the Bronze Age. The point has already been made that the moving of the bluestones has been remembered, but that it is a unique and momentous event, and in quite a different category from such apparently ephemeral matters as religion and social organization. However, there is backing from both literature and archaeology for the proposal that even these less definite matters may be remembered over an equally long time-span. Support from literature comes from traditions which parallel the spread of Indo-European languages to, among other places, India and the Celtic-speaking West. As Rees and Rees note,[59] there are 'striking similarities' between a group of stories told by the ancient Indians and those of other peoples whose languages are derived from the Indo-European. The similarities extend to social matters, for 'an account of the art, status, and conduct of Irish and Welsh court poets was described by an eminent orientalist as "almost a chapter in the history of India under another name".'[60] Other similarities are commented on by the same authors. For instance, the name of the goddess Danu, who figures in the Rig Veda, signifies 'stream' and 'the waters of heaven'. Her western counterparts, Danann in Ireland and Don in Wales (who is linked with Beli in Welsh tradition[61]), have names which are phonologically related, and the same root appears in the various English rivers called Don. Here are examples of social behaviour, and the name and an attribute of a deity, which have been recollected from the original Indo-European culture as it existed prior to its dispersal to the east and the west. There are, in fact, two instances of extended survival here, for there was independent survival of the same material in both branches. Archaeological support comes from archaic characteristics, recalling henges, of certain Iron Age hill-forts, and the deliberate siting of these hill forts over and around earlier Neolithic causewayed enclosures. It is thought that these may be indicative of the 'renaissance of early rites, involving occupation material and the dead, in Iron Age times'.[62]

It is to be noted that these instances of survival of tradition, both oral and archaeological, occur in the cultural milieu under observation, and they cover roughly the same period. Further enquiries can therefore be made without serious misgiving about the possibility of this sort of survival.

The tally of pagan associations presented by the three traditions of the moving of stones has by no means been completed. But from what has already been examined there emerges an intriguing possibility that the closely knit complex of pagan symbolism, linked with the floated and erected stones, represents both a substantial addition to what little we can recognize as Bronze Age 'literature' and also a description of the religious background to megalithic construction — perhaps even to that of the first stone structure of Stonehenge.

The associations of the moved or floated stones have up to now been peripheral to the main themes of the Arthurian cycle, but a point has been reached where the stones are to be linked with a central feature, thus paving the way for a general review of the relationship of Arthurian matters to paganism. There is one more common factor between two versions of the bluestone move to be considered, and that is the place of arrival. The stone with Balin's sword in it floated to the river beneath Camelot (Malory XIII 2) and the peron set up by Merlin was in the meadow by the river of Camelot (Malory X 2). This apparent association of Camelot with those floated or erected stones, which, it has been argued here, could be the bluestones of Stonehenge, might be written off as merely due to the attracting force of the prime Arthurian location, if it were not for the remarkable statement in the 'matter of Britain' to the effect that Camelot was the principal pagan site in the country and the place where the pagan king was crowned[63] (Sommer I 244). This suggestion of a location for a place as elusive as Camelot is at least worthy of consideration.

In case it should be mistakenly thought that the site of Camelot has already been decided, judging from the use of the name Camelot in association with Cadbury Castle in the title of the admirable account of the excavations there by Alcock, in the book *'By South Cadbury is that Camelot . . .': Excavations at Cadbury Castle 1966–1970*, this is by no means the view the author himself expresses. What Alcock actually says is: 'The truth is, however, that attempts to identify Camelot are pointless. The name, and the very concept of Camelot, are inventions of the French medieval poets.'[64] Now that the 'matter of Britain' has been shown to contain numerous references to sacred kingship, we know that the French medieval poets were not inventors of all the themes they used, but relied on tradition to a surprising extent. From this new viewpoint, even Camelot, like the most part of the romantic trappings of the Arthurian legend, may be seen to belong to the corpus of traditional material collected by twelfth-century folklorists. Alcock's forthright remarks merely indicate that, if there is more to be found out about Camelot, it is to the 'matter of Britain' that we must turn as a source. There, the original importance of Camelot is in the sphere of paganism, as noted above, and in the context of the shadowy realm of Sarras and the Sarrasen faith. We are told that the Sarrasens had a holy city: we are also told that the pagan kings of the Sarrasens were crowned at Camelot, which was the principal centre of idolatry in the realm. This might mean that the 'holy city of Sarras' and 'Camelot' are alternative descriptions of the same place. The romances never make this equation. They refer to Sarras as being 'in parts of Babylon' (Malory XVII 23), a very distant journey indeed from Britain in the Dark Ages. But there are one or two hints that Camelot and Sarras may have been the same, or at least part of the same pagan system. For, though Galahad's reign and death took place at Sarras, Camelot was the scene of his accession, for it was at Camelot that Galahad drew the sword from the stone, exactly as Arthur did in the better-known instance. The sword-drawing feat was in some way symbolic of Arthur's right to the throne of Logres; perhaps the same is indicated in the case of Galahad. But, for the purposes of the story, there could not be two kings at Camelot, so Galahad's accession would automatically be suppressed. The suppression, how-ever, was not complete. We are next told that Galahad, in honour of his highness, was led to the king's own chamber and slept in the king's bed (Malory XIII 8).

Whether the 'holy city' and Camelot are the same place or not, the pagan character of Galahad's actions at both places suggests a firm link between these two cities and the system of sacred kingship outlined in earlier chapters. At Camelot the arrival of the floated stone indicated the beginning of the Grail Quest (Malory XIII 2); the sword-drawing and

Galahad's assumption of his place in the Siege Perilous show his induction as a sacred king; he was, significantly, dressed in red, and he sent greeting to Pelles (a maimed king) and 'my lord Petchere' (i.e., pêcheur, the Fisher King); and after the drawing of Balin's sword, there was yet another indication of the close presence of a native Zeus when, at a night-time gathering, the assembled company heard the 'cracking and crying of thunder . . . [and] in the midst of this blast entered a sunbeam more clearer by seven times than ever they saw day . . .' (Malory XIII 7). Later, Galahad's female companion bleeds a dish of blood to heal a lady; he visits the castle of Carbonek (Corbenic in the French originals), where he sees the Grail Procession and anoints the Maimed King with the blood which drips from the spear; and finally he dies as king of Sarras and is buried there. In addition to these activities associated with Galahad, there was a sun-temple in the city of Sarras.[65]

The 'minster' that Galahad attended after the sword-drawing ceremony is presumably the principal church at Camelot referred to on another occasion as St Stephen's (Malory III 5). This dedication may preserve a recollection of a pagan festival. The relevance of 'the feast of Stephen' to the solstice, which it misses by a few days (but not as much as New Year's Day does), is never emphasized. But to a pagan observer of the skies, the year was born when the sun's decline was reversed at the winter solstice, and lengthening days gave promise of a new season of plenty. The Celtic year began on 1 November (Samhuin) and proceeded through the cross-quarter days 1 February, 1 May and 1 August, a calendar said to be particularly suitable for a pastoral people. But there are indications that in Megalithic times there was interest in the solstices and equinoxes. Certainly the axis of Stonehenge is oriented on the rising point of the midsummer sun (which, contrary to popular opinion, rose (and still rises) appreciably to the north of the Heelstone), the earliest feature showing this direction accurately being the first ring of tall stones, the original bluestone structure which was later dismantled but its stones used in other settings. A line which points to the rising sun at midsummer points also, in the other direction, to the setting sun at the winter solstice. This, to a pagan astronomer, might appear to be the turning point of the year. Would the sun continue to decline towards unending night, or could priestly intervention persuade it to retrace its steps? This may have seemed a more decisive moment than the corresponding situation at midsummer, and some commentators on Stonehenge have considered that the midwinter aspect of the axis (looking through the slot in the most magnificent feature in the whole composition, the great trilithon) may have been predominant in the later stages of its use.

I have drawn attention to Camelot (and to Sarras with its overlapping set of pagan associations) on account of the meadow or river of Camelot being the site of the 'peron' and the 'floated stone', which, for the reason outlined earlier, may be considered as distant echoes of the bluestones and their erection. We now find, in the immediate context of these stories of moved or floated stones, references to religious ancillaries – a sun-temple, the winter solstice, thunder and lightning – which are appropriate to the physical situation of Stonehenge or its likely circumstance in prehistory. Though it has not been suggested before, we should bear in mind as a real possibility that there is some sort of correspondence between, on the one hand, what tradition describes as the 'holy city of Sarras' and 'Camelot, the most important religious site and where the pagan kings were crowned', and on the other, the complex of megalithic monuments on Salisbury Plain which demonstrates the presence there of a religious centre of national importance.

The idea of Sarras as a name important at one time in British paganism may be generally unfamiliar, but it is supported by references in the 'matter of Britain' to 'the gods of the Sarrasins' (the Sarrasins or Sarrasens being the inhabitants of Sarras, frequently confused with Saracens). These gods (Sommer I 252) were 'Tervagant, Mahomme, Apolin and Jupiter'. It seems unlikely that the prophet of such a fiercely monotheistic religion as Islam would have been entirely happy in the company of this mixed trio of pagan deities. Mahommed (AD 570–632) can scarcely be supposed to have had any spiritual impact on Dark Age Britain and his presence on this list must be an artificial introduction, presumably following from the misconception that the inhabitants of Sarras were 'Saracens'. As far as the other three are concerned, Jupiter is equated in inscriptions with Taranis, a Celtic thunder god, and Apollo with Mabon son of Modron –

the divine youth, son of the divine mother. Tervagant (otherwise known as Terican) is elsewhere described as having a fountain shaded by three pines, from which the water flowed through a silver pipe on to a peron of marble and thence into a vessel of lead (Sommer V 89).

The name Sarras may have disappeared from our vocabulary, but the repercussions of its ancient religious importance have by no means faded away. The adjectival form may still cling to the prehistoric monuments of Salisbury Plain in the form *sarsen*. Dictionaries explain sarsen as equivalent to Saracen. As applied to the stones of Wiltshire, the name of the desert inhabitants of the Middle East cannot be directly relevant. It has therefore been suggested that the use of the word in the context of Stonehenge implies 'foreign', that is, brought from a distance. This explanation is not very likely as sarsens are common in the neighbourhood. Alternatively, the word could be used to mean pagan, as 'mahoumerie' is used to mean idolatry in the 'matter of Britain'. If so, it seems unlikely that the poets would have invented a matching name for the holy city of the traditional tales they were repeating. Perhaps the original name of the inhabitants of the holy city resembled 'Saracen', and so caused this particular synonym of 'pagan' to be used. There may have been a certain amount of assimilation to the name familiar in the Middle Ages as the epitome of paganism, but we may hope that the original name of the builders of the sarsen structures has survived without much alteration.

In an even more heavily disguised form than sarsen, Sarras may have entered into the national consciousness in an unexpected way, by a decisive influence on the form in which the early 'literature' has reached us. It is surprising that two different, and to outward appearances unconnected, traditions should have been misplaced into post-Roman times. Geoffrey of Monmouth mistakenly put his Giants' Dance story into the time of Aurelius Ambrosius, and the block of traditions concerning sacred kings, the gods Bran and Beli, etc., has intruded into the Arthurian sequence at a time which seems to be a generation or so later than the reign of Aurelius. Is it a coincidence that the same mistake has been made twice, or was there some directing influence which persuaded two authors in very different circumstances to fall into the same error? One possible influence which would have had this effect is the incorrect attribution of 'Joseph of Arimathea' to the middle of the first century, but there is also a more direct possibility. The name Saxon sometimes appears in the 'matter of Britain' in situations where it seems out of context. The usual form of the word for Saxons – Sesnes – seems to have been confused with Sarrasens. If we assume this mistake to have been made, and write Sarrasen back into the story of the Giants' Dance, the revised version, which would say that the stones were moved to commemorate the dead of the Sarrasen cult (which appears to have required the death of sacrificial victims in its holy city), makes much better sense than Geoffrey of Monmouth's original, which said the stones were moved to commemorate victims of the Saxons (killed on 1 May!). And in the other instance of a misplaced tradition, the affairs of Galahad and his system are closely bound up with Sarras and the Sarrasens and thus give plenty of scope for this simple misdirecting error, which has apparently resulted in widespread confusion between pre-Christian cult activities and the doings of an at least nominally Christian court of the fifth and sixth centuries A D.

Analysis of the 'matter of Britain' shows that more and more aspects of tradition can be allocated to the pagan complex so far outlined in these pages. It might be thought that the true Saxon element (if any) was being squeezed out by the Sarrasen and that this would distort the familiar story. Curiously enough, this does not, indeed cannot, happen, for the very simple reason that, as far as Malory is concerned, the Saxons are not there to be displaced. In the excellent index to the Medici edition (reprinted 1935), there is not a single reference to the Saxons. The whole majestic sweep of the Arthurian story, as we have known it in England for the last four centuries, proceeds to its sad conclusion without the Saxons playing any part in it, as if, indeed, it was oblivious of their existence. The same cannot be said of the Saracens (as Malory spells the name), for 40,000 of them attacked the eleven kings who had rebelled against Arthur (Malory I 18), and, of course, they were the inhabitants of the holy city, and as such chose Galahad as their king. Malory has suppressed all mention of the Saxons who appear in his sources, without, it seems, affecting the course of the story in any way. But by his time the cycle had been stabilized in its familiar form. It was too late to reverse the effect of the confusion between

Saxon and Sarrasen merely by omitting the former. This simple mistake had already resulted in the pagan deities, heroes and heroines of early Britain appearing at the court of King Arthur in the guise of kings and queens, knights and their ladies. This, coupled with the fortunate chance of French interest in the resulting combination, led to their survival – hence our possession of an unrivalled store of early 'literature' going back to the Bronze Age.

The key that gives meaning to what was previously obscure is the view of western European paganism put forward by Frazer. With its aid we have been able to recognize several aspects of pre-Christian religion as forming part of the 'matter of Britain'.

PART III

The Pagan Framework underlying the Arthurian Legend

7 The Birth of Arthur

This enquiry into Arthurian matters has produced several correspondences between aspects of pagan religion and episodes in the romances, and some characters in the romances seem to have pagan significance. This element of pre-Christian religion cannot have been introduced in the twelfth century; it must have been present in the sources of the poets who produced the 'matter of Britain'. Recollections of paganism in the romances tend to support other arguments in favour of the origin of this material in Celtic language oral tradition. These recollections may also give new information about British prehistory, in so far as they draw attention to the practice of various cults; their structure may cast light on the method of transmission from the original event to the romantic episode; and their presence in twelfth-century tales shows that early British literature has an unexpected degree of continuity with oral tradition.

The last of these effects will occupy the remainder of this book, in which the penetration of what are apparently pagan motifs into many aspects of the romances will be demonstrated. The structure of the pagan tradition will be analysed for what information it has to yield, but there are no substantial additions to be made to the cult practices already described. There is, however, one point which will interest the reader of literature originating from the 'matter of Britain'. The patterns of behaviour which have been observed in the chapters on sacred kingship often crop up in less complete forms. These eroded versions would be of no value in, say, making the comparison with the sequence of events at Nemi, because they contain too few of the diagnostic features. But now the point has been made that defending a ford or a fountain is reminiscent of a pagan activity, we can recognize this type of situation in less fully documented instances. We can even allow our interest to quicken at so attenuated an example of the formula as the knight who lay fully armed under a tree by a bubbling well (Malory X 2) and who fought

Sir Tristram there. In ordinary life, after all, men do not wait by springs for the opportunity of personal combat.

As far as the structure of the pagan tradition is concerned, our enquiry began with the assumption that the fame of the historical Arthur could have attracted 'into his orbit' the exploits of earlier heroes. Some such material has now been identified. It includes several types of sacred kingship; it specifies the names of deities, heroes and heroines; and it describes the ritual deaths and the ceremonials enacted by human participants. When we observe this pagan scene as a whole, there is an unexpected uniformity about it. The process of attraction might have been expected to produce a structureless hotch-potch. In contrast, the system of sacred kingship which appears to underlie the romances has a single unifying theme – the magical benefit thought to be derived from having a vigorous ruler – and the individuals involved belong to an inter-related group of deities and heroes.

If a self-contained mythological system – some sort of native pantheon and its practices – has been attracted into the Arthurian orbit, there is information to be gained from this situation, both about the method of transmission and the originating circumstances. The emphasis on pagan religion suggests that a religious community will have provided the principal means of transmission, and the substantial overlap with Geoffrey of Monmouth's Giants' Dance episode indicates that that recollection of the distant past was preserved in the same, or a closely linked, channel of communication. As the tradition has not become completely garbled, it probably had meaning to its hearers until comparatively late relative to written forms. This impression is reinforced by occasional clarity in the 'fine structure' of the tradition – the details of a procession, the comments of the bystanders, the names (or rather titles) of participants and the colours they wore. The colleges of chanting priests would have disappeared many centuries before, but as long as people retained a memory of paganism, so that the tales struck a chord of superstitious awe, the corpus of traditional tales would tend to maintain its integrity.

The circumstance which now calls for attention is that a tradition which has survived into this millennium apparently refers to an event which happened about 2000 BC. There is nothing out of the ordinary here. It is natural for religions to look back to the acts of their founding fathers, and there is evidence for cultural continuity over the intervening period – a continuity which followed a substantial reorientation in the centuries immediately before the bluestone move. Because the tradition covers such a long period, we shall have to examine in some detail indications in it which suggest historical sequence. The usual method of calculation by means of generations is not available because, in the romances, being a son or daughter seems to imply religious allegiance, not the natural relationship; and the names are of offices, which may have continued with consecutively replaced participants for considerable periods. But there are several occasions on which reference is made to earlier events, sometimes to be measured in centuries before.

The clearest example of historical perspective in the 'matter of Britain' is the early date given to the arrival of Joseph 'of Arimathea'. This stands out from the usual practice of stringing episodes in sequence to give a coherent narrative, and has at least the appearance of portraying an event which preceded Arthur's reign by some centuries.

This enigmatic personage came to Britain, it is said, at a time when it was entirely populated by Sarrasens and unbelievers, and its principal and most holy city was Camelot (Sommer I 212, 244). Joseph brought with him the grail, and presumably the ritual of the grail procession, and among his companions was Bron, who officiated at a ceremonial fish meal (Sommer I 251) and so acquired the title of 'Rich Fisher'. From Joseph's immediate entourage sprang the lines of descent of both Launcelot and Elaine, the parents of the principal grail hero. Joseph's adventures, both before and after reaching this country, are of a missionary cast. Large numbers of Sarrasens (15,000) are said to have been 'converted' by him at Sarras, and 1500 at Camelot by his son and successor, Josephe, who, because of the similarity of name, is not always easy to distinguish from him. Their most notable 'convert' was King Evelake of Sarras who, when he attempted to approach the grail (Sommer I 241), became preserved, covered in wounds (according to Malory) until such time as he should be healed by the successful grail-seeker. In due course, after the deaths of Joseph and Josephe, the grail passed into the keeping of Alain, the twelfth son of Bron, who took it to the Terre Foraine where Galaphes (who had taken the name Alphasan on his 'conversion') built the castle of Corbenic to hold it. After the death of Alphasan in the manner already described, the grail passed to a line of grail-keepers – Aminadap, Catheloys, Manaal and Lambor – all surnamed the Rich Fisher. Lambor was the father of Pellehan, the father of Pelles whose daughter Elaine was the mother of Galahad.

It is generally supposed that 'traditions' of this sort, claiming knowledge of personal and national origins, have about as much relevance to history as *Just So Stories* to biology. So any argument to the contrary is bound to be advanced with caution. Yet, in the context of material which is known to contain the remains of a genuine pagan tradition, it seems reasonable enough to ascribe the rituals of the grail-procession and the fish meal to a pagan cult brought to Britain at some specific but unfortunately indeterminate time in the past.

The matter is clinched by the extremely firm association between the dramatis personae of this presumed traditional account of the arrival of the grail cult and the styles of sacred kingship described earlier.

Joseph 'of Arimathea' himself was wounded in the thigh with a sword (Sommer I 253).

Josephe was wounded in the thigh with a spear by an angel (Sommer I 77).

Bron and the Fisher Kings (as the Rich Fishers are also called) owe their origin to the Welsh Bran,[66] a deity associated with wounding and decapitation.

Evelake, blinded and wounded, 'lived three hundred winters this holy life' (Malory XIV 4).

Galaphes died after being struck between the thighs by a fiery man (Sommer I 289).

Lambor was the recipient of the Dolorous Stroke (Sommer I 290).

Pellehan was wounded in the thighs in a battle and so became known as the maimed king (Sommer I 290).

Pelles, the maimed king, was wounded through the thighs when he drew a sword from its scabbard in a magic ship (Malory XVII 5).

The principal site of these activities was the Terre Foraine, which as a result of the Dolorous Stroke became the Terre Gaste, that is, the Waste Land.

It seems improbable that a concocted account of an imaginary past, made up in the twelfth century, would have been constructed with so much care as to include supporting detail of the right kind. There can be little doubt that the 'matter of Britain' contains the tail end of a genuine tradition about the arrival of an important cult, a tradition which carries with it a great deal of information about the original event.

Unfortunately there seems little in the account of Joseph's arrival to indicate the date, or to tie the cult to a known archaeological culture (but see Appendix I). However, there is a strong suggestion of sequence, in that the affairs of Joseph are invariably described as being earlier than those of Galahad by a period which, when it is stated, is measured in centuries. Although the length of the period can be discounted, the suggestion that Joseph was appreciably earlier than Galahad leads to an interesting conclusion, for there is just a chance that the supremacy of the Galahad cult can be, if not actually dated, at least allotted a position in a prehistorical sequence. A 'Galahad', not the familiar son of Launcelot, nor Launcelot's grandfather, but a much earlier Galahad who was a son of Joseph of Arimathea, was given the country which is now called Wales to rule. At that time the country's name was Hocelice or Hosseliche (Sommer I 282), but on Galahad's death it was renamed Gales in his honour. Since other examples occur at this particular language interface of proper names which turn up in French sources with an initial 'G', but in English with a 'W',* this is an explanation of how Wales got its name! Fictitious name-giving founders are a common enough currency, but a near neighbour, Ireland, does have a name which could be derived from a deity, and Galahad comes from a pagan background, so let us at least see where the attribution of the name of Wales to a cult figure will lead us if it is genuine.

Gales, still today Pays de Galles to the French, is, as the name of a Celtic-speaking country, a parallel to those other one-time Celtic provinces whose names have the same sequence of sounds: Galicia in northern Spain, Galatia in Asia Minor, and, less obviously, Gaul. These Gal- names correspond to the names Keltoi and Galli by which the

*Gawain and Walwain for an individual, Terre Gaste and the Waste Land for a country.

Greeks and Romans knew the tribes that, in historical times, were pressing into their own spheres of influence from the Celtic heartlands north of the Alps.

That these names should be more or less the same shows that they are from the vocabulary of the invaders, a name they would have used of themselves. A certain amount of uniformity is implied, but what, in real terms, does this uniformity represent? First of all, not racial homogeneity. Although an early form of Celtic culture, with language as a most important component, may at some indeterminate time in the past have been the unique possession of a limited group of people living in comparative isolation, it was to spread, over many centuries, until, at the height of its influence, it covered several countries and provinces. In this expansion the racial stock of 'original Celts' would inevitably have been diluted and absorbed into the more numerous indigenous populations. However far this process had gone at the time under consideration, the point can safely be made that racial purity would not have been an essential constituent of the underlying unity represented by the 'Gal-' names. Far more important would have been cultural factors, represented today partly by the style of material remains and partly by less concrete matters such as the survival of Celtic languages and evidence of Celtic beliefs. In the latter category one of the most striking examples is the scatter of 'nemeton' place names, implying the worship of the sacred grove. Apart from several instances each in Britain and France, there are Drunemeton in Galatia in Asia Minor and Nemetobriga in Spanish Galicia – neatly underlining the correspondence between this particular cult and the spread of Gal- names. Other religious features widely scattered are: the practice of depositing treasure in water (the cult of sacred waters reached a peak of popularity in Iron Age times); the river names which come from the same root as the names of the western goddesses Danann and Don – Danube, Dnieper, Dniester and the Russian and English Dons;[67] the coincidence of the names of 'the gods Brennos and Bolgios leading their peoples into Macedonia in the third century BC'[68] with similar names in Western tradition; and the popularity of inscriptions in Gaul to the god Belenus, whose name is reminiscent of names in the Western tradition. The religious elements of the Celtic spread are clearly also ingredients of the cult pattern of the 'matter of

Britain', so it is not at all surprising that a figure from this background (particularly one closely associated with sacred waters) should have universal popularity in the Celtic domains, even to the extent that it is by his name that these countries are now remembered, including Wales.

A look at the Welsh population gives point to the comments made above about the dilution of 'original Celts', at least in peripheral areas. Ammianus Marcellinus, 'who wrote in Byzantium in the sixth century, but who derived his material from Timagenes, a writer in the reign of Augustus', described the Gauls as nearly all 'of a lofty stature, fair and of ruddy complexion'.[69] Remembering that the present-day Welsh are the descendants of the people common to that country and the rest of southern Britain in Roman times, and that there has been no substantial replacement by migration into Wales during the intervening period, these are the last features which one would expect to be picked out as characteristic of the bulk of the people of Roman Britain. The reason is that these native British, although Celtic speaking, were to a large extent the descendants of the Neolithic 'first-farmers' – the first inhabitants to produce food on a scale to allow the country to support a substantial population – and so tend to conform to the 'Mediterranean' type, described by J. Geipel in *The Europeans* as short and dark, with long heads, narrow faces and a high average level of blood group 'O'. The absence of large-scale immigration since the first farmers is confirmed by field studies. P. Ashbee, speaking of southern Britain in the period from the Neolithic to 'the threshold of Roman times' says that 'Beakers, just before the beginning of the second millennium BC, and what appear to have been minor influxes in Iron Age times, were our only archaeologically detectable invasions'[70]. Yet at the end of the period Celtic speech was general in the south, though in the north the aborigines continued to speak the original pre-Celtic, perhaps, indeed, pre-Indo-European, tongue – Pictish, which remained in use for many centuries to come. In view of the evidence for continuity of population, the introduction of a new language later than 2000 BC may best be explained by the incursion of relatively few individuals, whether by way of trade, missionary effort or a military aristocracy.

Here, then, is the background to the change in name of Wales from Hocelice to Gales, but the time at which this took place remains to be discussed. Obviously, the first choice will be that indicated by the invasions which left the names Galicia and Galatia, both of which names faithfully reproduce the structure 'Gal-s'. These invasions took place in 450 BC and about 270 BC, respectively. Though there is no evidence for a comparable invasion in Wales, the parallels are exact enough to carry considerable weight. But this argument is not exclusive of an earlier date for Wales. There can be no suggestion that Gal- names sprang up at this time, any more than that Celtic culture was a sudden new arrival. The name is just as likely to be coeval with the origin of Celtic speech as with the cultural apparatus of the Iron Age, and it is possible that the people of the Urnfield culture of about 1300 to 700 BC 'already spoke a recognizably Celtic language'.[71] And religious tradition is so tenacious that this particular strand might even, like the Don names, stem from the earliest arrival of Indo-European culture. The matter cannot be decided with certainty, but an Iron Age date would be the safest guess for the change of name. Whatever the date, there is the intriguing possibility that the pre-Celtic name of Wales has not been forgotten.

To extract as much information as possible from the element of time-scale in the 'matter of Britain' we should also examine another situation where there is a suggestion of sequence. Prior to Arthur's reign the important figures were Vortigern, Aurelius Ambrosius, Uther Pendragon and, above all, Merlin. What does this mean in terms of the pagan tradition which is a constant feature of the material?

The story is, briefly, as follows: Vortigern, who had usurped the throne of Britain, attempted to build a tower but whatsoever the masons 'wrought one day was all swallowed up by the soil the next'. His wizards told him that to ensure its stability a 'lad that had never had a father' should be killed and his blood sprinkled over the mortar and stones. In due course, the king's agents discovered at Carmarthen the youthful Merlin, who qualified for the office of sacrifice because his mother, of noble birth, had been impregnated by a devil in the shape of a man in a locked room. Merlin, supernaturally precocious, saved his own life by providing a solution which did not require human sacrifice. Vortigern then unwisely called for the assistance of the Saxons in his internal wars. When they turned against him, he was unable to displace them. However, the rightful heir to the throne, Aurelius Ambrosius, eventually regained it with the help of his brother, Uther Pendragon, and had some success against the Saxons. During Vortigern's reign a group of British nobles had been treacherously slain by the Saxons near the monastery of Ambrius, not far from Salisbury, on the Kalends of May. To provide a suitable memorial for them, Merlin and Uther were sent to fetch the Giants' Dance and re-erect it on Salisbury Plain. Aurelius Ambrosius was buried there on his death and his brother Uther came to the throne.

Uther commissioned Merlin to construct the Round Table at Cardoel in Wales (Sommer II 54). It was inaugurated on the following Pentecost (alternatively, Whitesuntide) and a company of fifty knights was selected by Merlin to sit at it. After a prototype which Joseph of Arimathea had constructed to hold the grail, the new table had a 'dreaded seat', used in the original by Josephe, which had the capacity to destroy any unauthorized user. At this time, Uther ordained that the festivals of Christmas, Whitsuntide and All Saints were to be kept at Cardoel. Uther then fell in love with Igerne, or as Malory spells it, Igraine, the wife of a Cornish duke. She resisted his advances and fled with the duke. War broke out between the two parties, and Igerne was besieged in the heavily defended castle of Tintagel. However, Merlin by enchantment transformed Uther into the likeness of the duke and so obtained for him access to Igerne. As a result, Arthur was conceived. But an hour or two before this had happened, the duke had been killed elsewhere on the field of battle. So, when Uther later married Igerne, he was able to claim the child as his legitimate heir. As a reward for his part in the affair, however, Merlin was allowed to bring up the heir to the throne, and we hear nothing more of Arthur until after Uther's death.

Before exploring the ways in which these events correspond to the pagan scenes described earlier, we need to look at the characteristics of heroes in Celtic literature. The 'natural history' of this larger-than-life type of individual is described by Rees and Rees in *Celtic Heritage* where, for example, they list the most striking features of a hero's birth.[72] In what were 'originally religious stories', we find that, 'whether the hero has an earthly father or not, he is usually begotten by another – a king, a man from another race or a supernatural being', and again, 'The hero is more often than not conceived "illegitimately" . . . , if the mother is married, he is begotten through what would normally be called adultery, and the irregularity of the union is often accentuated by violence and trickery'.[73] It will be seen that the births of both Arthur and Merlin conform to this general pattern, and are, in fact, referred to by Rees and Rees in their discussion on the births of heroes.[74] The births of other personages in the 'matter of Britain', such as Galahad and Mordred, also conform. Indeed, the French tradition provides what might be an interesting addition to our knowledge of the birth of heroes from Welsh literary sources. It does so by describing an event which could be the real-life original of some of the stories in this group. Helayne le Blank, a hero whose future greatness had been foretold, was fathered at an annual festival by the winner of a tournament (who had to be persuaded by supernatural means to perform the act) on the daughter of a god, Bran, described in this instance as Brangoire. The 'matter of Britain' has here preserved the recollection of a situation which would explain several of the unusual features of the births of Celtic heroes. The circumstances of the birth of Helayne give chapter and verse for what Rees and Rees describe in general terms only: 'widespread rituals by which supernatural powers were given access to women through the agency of such human personifications as kings, priests or strangers'.[75] Traces of ritual involving copulation also persist in such traditions as that of King Conchobar, who was regarded as a terrestrial god and 'was entitled to the first night with the bride of every Ulsterman',[76] but in no case is the begetting of a hero attributed to the practice of 'jus primae noctis'.

Uther, then, is connected with paganism by his name which, according to C. Squire, links him with Bran; by his association with the bluestone move; and by his inauguration of the Round Table, with its close association with the grail and other characteristics which imply that its ambience is pagan. In addition, he fathered a hero on Igerne, who herself brings a train of pagan associations. As well as being the mother of Arthur, she had three daughters, Morgan, Morgawse and Elaine. The first of these is described as a goddess. She was also patroness of the otherworld realm of Avalon and she married King Uriens of Gore, possibly another form of the god Bran. The second married King Lot of Orkney, in whom we may reasonably see the Celtic god Lludd[77] thinly disguised. The third is not characterized, but the name Elaine may well be significant in the context of the 'matter of Britain'.

So the birth of Arthur (or whoever the original hero whose characteristics Arthur has shouldered may have been) was heralded by pagan trumpets on all sides.

8 The Sword in the Stone

By the time Uther died, Arthur was a young man, but neither he nor his foster parents knew the secret of his birth, and the existence of an heir to the throne was unknown to all except Merlin. The matter was resolved by the appearance in the churchyard of the greatest church in London, against the high altar, of 'a great stone four square, like unto a marble stone; and in midst thereof was like an anvil of steel a foot on high, and therein stuck a fair sword naked by the point, and letters there were written in gold about the sword that said thus:– Whoso pulleth out this sword of this stone, is rightwise king born of all England' (Malory I 5). Arthur established his right to the throne by being the only person able to draw the sword, but he had to demonstrate his capacity several times, at New Year's Day, at Twelfth Night, at Candlemas, at Easter and finally at Pentecost before, on the last occasion, he was crowned. Even then he was not universally accepted and came into conflict with the rulers of the smaller kingdoms which made up his realm. Within a year of his accession there was an insurrection by six kings – Lot of Lothian and Orkney, Uriens of Gore, Nentres of Garlot (the husbands of Arthur's three step-sisters), the king of Scotland, the king with the Hundred Knights, and the king of Carados – which Arthur only succeeded in suppressing because of the brilliant light cast by his sword Excalibur (Malory I 9).

Merlin now warned Arthur that he needed support and advised him to send for King Ban of Benwick and his brother King Bors of Gaul. Meanwhile the six kings also received reinforcements from the Duke of Cambenet, King Brandegoris of Stranggore, King Clariance of Northumberland, King Idres of Cornwall and King Cradelmas of North Wales. War between the two factions began and the eleven kings were defeated at Bedegraine with the help of Ban and Bors. The rebels withdrew to King Uriens's city of Sorhaute, where they heard that their own countries were being overrun by 'Saracens' (Malory I 18) or, as the *Vulgate* has it, Saxons (Sommer II 125). At this point the courses of the *Vulgate* and

Morte Darthur diverge. According to the former, the rebel kings, under pressure from a common enemy, came to terms with Arthur, whereupon Merlin organized a meeting of peoples of many languages on Salisbury Plain, to which Arthur's allies were invited as well as the eleven kings and their supporters (Sommer II 376). At this meeting, Arthur was acknowledged as paramount, thus ushering in the golden age of knight errantry and the Round Table. In Malory the opposing parties do not come to terms. The eleven kings and Rience of North Wales, a late arrival to the confederation, were defeated and were all killed with the help of the brothers Balin and Balan. They were buried in the church of St Stephen's in Camelot, 'and the remnant of knights and others were buried in a great rock' (Malory II 10). But the result in terms of Arthur's supremacy is the same.

The story of the sword drawn from the stone has intrigued readers for centuries, but whether it is pure fancy, or whether some matter-of-fact explanation lies behind it, has never been resolved. We can, however, be reasonably certain that the sword itself is not an invention of the French medieval poets, for Malory's 'Excalibur' and Geoffrey of Monmouth's 'Caliburn' (Caliburnus in the Latin original) are merely late forms of a name which is more accurately recollected in Welsh tradition as 'Caledvwlch'. The existence of this sword in the underlying tradition, and the correctness of the Welsh version of its name, are vouched for by the presence of a parallel in Irish tradition – another sword, 'Caladbolg', which has a name closely resembling that of the Welsh sword. Since, in Welsh, 'b' slips easily into 'v', and 'w' has the sound of an 'o', the correspondence is closer than the immediate appearance of the names suggests.

CALADBOLG
CALEDVWLCH

O'Rahilly, in *Early Irish History and Mythology*, points out that the second element of this name, -bolg, means lightning. This designation strongly suggests that the sword belongs to the category of weapon signifying the thunderbolt or lightning, well-known as the attributes of Zeus and Thor. The class is a broad one, and as well as axe and hammer includes spear and sword – often described as fiery. The concept was widespread, and its many survivals show it to have retained a considerable hold on later generations. One such survival can be identified in the 'matter of Britain', now that the association of the sword with lightning has been pointed out. It was the *light* shining from Excalibur which enabled Arthur to defeat the six kings. However the association with Arthur may have arisen, and whatever the drawing of the sword from the stone may signify, the shining sword has a basis in the underlying tradition as the attribute of a native Zeus.

From the sword itself we now turn to the act of drawing a sword from a stone. There is another instance of this, in which Galahad drew Balin's sword from the stone which Merlin had floated to Camelot, and so inaugurated the Grail Quest and his own year-long reign at the Holy City. There are several correspondences here. In both instances a sword is drawn from a stone at Pentecost as the precursor of a reign. And in the case of Balin's sword, a good deal is known about the mythological background: this act was clearly of great significance, for it carries with it

1 the pagan association of Balin:
   the king of Ireland's son slain at Merlin's peron; the Dolorous Stroke, maiming the king and resulting in the waste land; the damsel who bled a dish of blood in his company; the combat with the red defender of the island.
2 The pagan associations of the floated stones.
3 The pagan associations of the Grail Quest:
   its introduction to the Terre Foraine by Josephe; the building of the Grail Castle by Alphisem; the night adventures in the Grail Castle; and (linking with those of Balin) the healing of the maimed king and the bleeding of another damsel.

So the two instances of swords drawn from stones have considerable mythological interest, one for the association with lightning in the name and behaviour of the sword, the other for the associations listed above. But the associations of Balin's sword do not include a direct reference to lightning to make the correspondence complete. However, several of these associations are linked with lightning in ways which suggest that this particular mythological explanation will be appropriate. The devastation caused by the Dolorous Stroke is likened to the effect of lightning which had run everywhere;[78]

117

the donor of the wound between the thighs is, in the case of Alphisem, a fiery man, and in the case of Josephe, his countenance was bright as lightning,[79] the weapon which struck the victim in the night adventure in the Grail Castle is described as fiery or with a flaming pennon; Galahad's red clothing when he drew Balin's sword from the stone is explained (Sommer VI 57) as resembling the colour of fire, and so being appropriate to the occasion of Pentecost, when the Holy Ghost descended upon the disciples in the semblance of fire; and later in the same day the Holy Grail appeared, preceded by thunder and a brilliant light. Though, in our incomplete tradition, the sword of Balin is never described as shining, the rumble of thunder and the flash of lightning are constant presences in the background when it is about. We shall be justified in adding 'an association with the lightning cult' to the list of similarities between the two swords.

O'Rahilly makes another interesting comment linking '-bolg' with Welsh tradition. He traces the name of the Welsh god, Beli, via an Indo-European root 'bhel', meaning flash, to '-bolg;. So we have 'Excalibur' (=Caledvwlch/Caladbolg), a sword with the significant element of its name linked with Beli, paralleled by Balin's sword. This coincidence of name and function suggests that these two figures, Beli and Balin, may both be surviving representatives of the same native British lightning god.

If the sword has the characteristics of a pagan symbol, then it is to be expected that the act of drawing it would have been a symbolic gesture. When we look behind the medieval embellishments, such as the letters of gold saying 'Whoso pulleth out this sword . . . is rightwise king born of all England', we find that the transmitters of the story have confused effect with cause. What we are observing is not a test but a demonstration, by a ritual act performed at religious festivals, of the status of a sacred king selected for other reasons, perhaps at birth.

Exactly what springtime festival underlies Pentecost in this account is difficult to say. One possibility is Beltain, 1 May (or its eve), because it is linked, in name at least, with Belenus, presumed to be the Balin of the 'matter of Britain'. The main sequence of sword drawing rituals might well have taken place as follows:

Occasion		Notional Date
New Year's Day	Solstice	1 January
Candlemas	Cross-quarter day	1 February
'Easter'	Equinox	1 April
'Pentecost'	Cross-quarter day	1 May

The suggested relationship between the cross-quarter days and astronomical time assumes that they derive from a system using a twelve-month year, and that the present interval between the solstice and New Year's Day has no significance, being merely an error in some earlier reconciliation between the calendar and the course of the sun.

The series of wars against the rebel kings is another instructive feature of the Arthurian story. When the protagonists are examined closely, they give evidence of a good deal of repetition and overlapping. It appears as if, typically of the material, a single original circumstance was recollected in several apparently diverse traditions. When the traditions were gathered together in the twelfth century, what had originally been one event was regarded as a progressive series. Arthur's wars are distinguished by the presence of pagan deities on both sides. On Arthur's behalf Bran appears as King Ban and Beli as Balin. On the other side Lot has been suggested to derive from the god Lludd, and Bran appears again as Brandegoris of Stranggore (which can be analysed as Bran of Gore of Strong Gore). The widespread and inconsequential appearances of the name Bran in varying forms have already been commented on. Newstead's authoritative contribution, referred to on p. 74 above, traced the appearances of Bran in the romances as a whole. In the more limited sector of *Morte Darthur*, a precursor in the same field, Charles Squire, has made some interesting comments in *Celtic Myth and Legend*.[80] He quotes Sir Edward Strachey as saying that Malory 'has built a great, rambling, mediaeval castle, the walls of which enclose rude and even ruinous work of earlier times . . . .'. Squire goes on to say:

How rude and ruinous these relics were Malory doubtless had not the least idea, for he has completely jumbled the ancient mythology . . . the same dieties, under very often only slightly varying names, come up again and again as totally different characters.

Take, for example, the ancient deity of death and Hades. As King Brandegore, or Brandegoris (Brân of Gower), he brings five thousand mounted men to oppose King Arthur; but, as Sir Brandel, or Brandiles (Brân of Gwales), he is a valiant knight of the Round Table, who dies fighting in Arthur's service. Again, under his name of Uther Pendragon (Uther Ben) [i.e. the wonderful severed head], he is Arthur's father; though as King Ban of Benwyck (the 'Square Enclosure', doubtless the same as Taliesin's *Caer Pedryvan* and Malory's *Carbonek*), he is a foreign monarch, who is Arthur's ally. Yet again, as the father of Guinevere, Ogyrvran has become Leodegrance. [Ogyrvran or Ogyrfran could be a compound of the name Bran in which the 'B' has softened according to a Welsh grammatical rule known as lenition.] As King Uriens, or Urience, of Gore (Gower), he marries one of Arthur's sisters, fights against him, but finally tenders his submission, and is enrolled among his knights. Urien may also be identified in the *Morte Darthur* as King Rience, or Ryons, of North Wales. . . . while, to crown the various disguises of this proteus of British gods, he appears in an isolated episode as Balan, who fights with his brother Balin until they kill one another.

There is substantial agreement between Newstead and Squire, but whereas the former has surveyed a wider field, the latter has exploited further the possibility that there are forms in which 'F' or 'V' replaces 'B', as in Evrain in Newstead's list. Quite apart from lenition, the distinction between 'B' and 'V' is comparatively slight in several languages, and a transference from one to the other is not unknown. In a Celtic context, the alternative names of Ireland, Hibernia and Ivernia, and of the river, Severn and Sabrina, show how early written forms tended to preserve a 'B' against native 'V'.

Where Squire's conclusions extend Newstead's, they tend to be supported by the analysis of the romances in this book. Uther Pendragon is the 'father' of a hero, Arthur, in the sense referred to on p. 113; he is instrumental in fetching the Giants' Dance and in the defeat of the king of Ireland not far from Prescelly; and he commissions Merlin to make the Round Table after a prototype brought by Joseph of Arimathea for the grail. Uriens is 'married' to a goddess, Morgan le Fay; he is the father of the 'challenge knight', Owein; and he is said to be king of Gore, as Bran is in 'Brandegoris'. What little we know of Uriens thus tends to support the argument from his name that he (and hence the other characters bearing truncated versions of the same name) are equivalents of Bran.

Newstead's sources are closer to the original oral tradition, and by their greater detail and wider range amply support Squire's contention that Bran appears, under slightly differing names, as a large number of characters in stories derived from the 'matter of Britain'.

One possible explanation of finding Bran on both sides is that the compiler of the story, wishing to give weight to a rather sparse tradition, added names taken at random from a limited stock of characters. On the other hand, it can now be seen that the 'ancient mythology' is not necessarily as 'jumbled' in Malory as Squire thought. For Arthur (or rather his precursor) to have had a god for his father is quite in line with what is to be expected of heroes. And if Guenevere is in the same position, that too has parallels. And since we find Bran a deity in many widely spread localities, it may well have happened that his subjects came into conflict, and even changed sides. But as the possibility of random additions exists, it would be a mistake to read too much into the religious wars that marked Arthur's coming to power. All we can say with certainty is that the numerous occurrences of Bran in the story emphasize his original importance.

The pair Balan and Balin mentioned by Squire conform to the pattern already pointed out that the gods Bran and Beli tend to appear as brothers, with their original divinity forgotten, in the 'matter of Britain' and associated material. But Bran, as King Ban, is also described as the brother of King Bors in circumstances where the actions of these 'brothers' appear to parallel those of Balan and Balin. Who, it may be asked, was King Bors? Malory has little to say of him, but calls him king of Gaul. The *Vulgate*, however, is more informative. There he is, under names which are variants of Bohors or Boors, the king of Gannes in Little Britain and, as well as being King Ban's brother, he is married to Evaine, the sister of Ban's wife, Elaine. His son is the Sir Bors who, having been victorious in an annual tournament, fathered Helaine le Blank on Brangoire's daughter (Bran again) and later accompanied Galahad to Sarras. Though it has been suggested, by Squire, that King Bors was a god, there does not seem much to go on here. But there are one or two slight indications of deity. He is described as 'king' and his hero son as 'sir'. This, though of course not diagnostic, conforms to the standard pattern of relationship between god and hero in the 'matter of Britain'. Other examples are King Ban (Bran) and Sir Lancelot; King Pellinore (Beli) and Sir Percival; King Uriens (Bran) and Sir Owein, and King Baudemagus (Bran, again) and Sir Meleagant. Our analysis of sacred kingship has thus provided an appropriate background to the late nineteenth-century suggestion that Bors, or Emrys or Myrddin (that is, Merlin) are one and the same, and an equivalent of Zeus.[81] Behind this suggestion is the proposition that Bors and Emrys are words descending from a common stock. This is not so far-fetched as it might seem, for there is an equivalent of Emrys in Ambrosius, another title of Merlin. This has the consonant structure MBRS, from which the structures of Emrys, MRS, and Bors, BRS, can be derived by the omission of a letter. Exactly this sort of erosion can be shown to have occurred in other similar words. The character called Lambor[82] in the *Vulgate* appears as Labor in Malory, showing how an M can disappear from the sequence MBR; and the town of Amesbury derives from an original Ambr's Burg, showing how a B can disappear from the same group of letters. As well as having the consonant structure of Emrys-Bors-Ambrosius, these two words which have degraded in what seems to be the same way are very close to our theme in other respects. Lambor is a Fisher-King, a descendant of Galaphes (Sommer I 289) and himself the recipient of the dolorous stroke (which turned his country into the Waste Land), and he is the father of the Maimed King; and Amesbury is the place nearest to Stonehenge.

Arguments which depend on the shape of words are never very satisfactory, but this particular one leads to two attractive speculations. One is that if Merlin was a god this would explain his involvement with the moving of the blue-stones and his character of magician and shapeshifter. (He appeared on one occasion in the guise of a stag, most appropriately for a local Zeus since in the north-west of Europe stag-headed figures often carry the axe symbolic of thunder.) The other is that the links between the British sacred kings and Stonehenge are strengthened. Merlin-Ambrosius and Stonehenge are firmly linked by Geoffrey of Monmouth's account of the moving of the Giants' Dance; we now find the same root Ambr at Amesbury and the alternative form Bors sounds like the name used by Hecateus in his description of Stonehenge, when he speaks of Boreas as the ancestor of the Boreades, the priests of Stonehenge. The name the Greeks heard as Boreas might very well have been the name which has come down to us by word of mouth as Bors. It would not be unlikely for them to have assimilated the original name to a word which had meaning to them – the North Wind – particularly as, in this instance, the local cult activity included attempts at weather-control.

If this guess is right, then the hero Sir Bors would correspond to a priestly descendant of the local thunder and weather god of Stonehenge, Merlin-Ambrosius. So we can also guess that at some time long ago, not necessarily the period of Hecateus, the cult activities which took place there were those we can deduce from the story of Bors. His father was a god, so he was a child of the temple; he was brought up by the Lady of the Lake; he accompanied the successful grail-achiever Galahad during his year of kingship at Sarras; he won a tournament at Brangoire's castle and as a result was formally bedded with a priestess, Bran's daughter, upon whom he fathered a hero of the next generation; he suffered a 'night adventure' in which, his usefulness as a procreator over, he was struck by the 'lightning spear' of the god and finally carried away with his legs tied to the shafts of the demeaning cart, emasculated, jeered at by the crowd, and pelted with filth, offal and old shoes.

9 The Round Table

During the campaign against the rebel kings, Arthur went to the assistance of King Leodegan of Carmelide (or, as Malory has it, Leodegrance of Cameliard), who was being attacked by Rions or Rience, variously described as King of Yrelande, of Danemarche and Yrelande, of the Isles, and, by Malory, of North Wales. While in Caroaise, Leodegan's capital city, Arthur met Guenever for the first time and in due course a marriage between them was arranged by Merlin. For a dowry Leodegan provided the Round Table which had earlier been given to him by Uther Pendragon. Merlin brought Guenever to Camelot, and with her the Round Table and its company of a hundred knights. Since the full capacity of the table was one hundred and fifty knights, more knights were elected, including the only ones named at this stage: Gawaine, son of King Lot; Tor, son of King Pellinore; and King Pellinore himself. The wedding of Arthur and Guenever at St Stephen's, Camelot, was the occasion of a high feast, but while the knights were sitting at the Round Table waiting for it to begin, Merlin forecast a strange and marvellous adventure. At this moment a white hart ran into the hall pursued by a small white hound called a brachet and 'thirty couple of black running hounds' (Malory III 5). The brachet bit the hart which gave a great leap and overthrew a knight who then picked up the brachet, took horse, and rode away with it. At once a lady rode in on a white palfrey demanding that the king recover the brachet for her, but he had scarcely time to reply before she was seized by a fully armed knight and carried away by force. Merlin now warned that these events were significant and unless the king retrieved the participants it would bring dishonour to himself and his feast. Gawaine was therefore sent to fetch the hart, Tor the brachet and the knight, and Pellinore the lady and the knight; in case the knights should not willingly come, they were to be slain. The knights of the Round Table successfully carried out their tasks and returned to Camelot with stories of a challenge at a river crossing, a challenge where a horn was blown, and a severed head by a well, but the significance of the white hart, the white brachet and the abducted lady is never explained. The strange adventures which characterized the Arthurian court had begun.

It is the oddness of episodes like this which make the Arthurian scene unique. Other royal households of the Dark Ages no doubt had doughty champions comparable with the knights of the Round Table as far as martial prowess was concerned, but, except in the Celtic west, their adventures can scarcely have been so difficult to explain in terms of the natural world. This is what makes the Round Table so interesting. In whatever way we look a it – as a table with a significant perilous seat, as the setting for 'marvels' enacted on days of festival, or as a brotherhood of knights with a unique capacity for meeting strange adventures – it is out of the ordinary. Is the strangeness a matter of the supernatural – that is, of recollected paganism – and if so, can we recognize the styles of paganism as those which have already been found in the 'matter of Britain'?

As far as the construction and location of the table are concerned, it is easy enough to demonstrate links with paganism. It was made by Merlin, a key figure in another piece of religious construction, for Uther Pendragon (suggested to be an equivalent of Bran), after a prototype brought by Joseph of Arimathea, and given by Uther to Leodegrance (apparently another form of Bran). It was erected at what we can deduce from its name, Cardoel, to have been a notable pagan site. Cardoel (or Cardol, Carduel and so on – the name is variously spelt and even more wildly attributed to present-day places) was the 'caer', which in names derived from Welsh commonly means town or fort, of one Do or Dos or Doon, the 'forester' of Uther and the father of Giflet, a knight of the Round Table who, as Malory's Griflet le Fise de Dieu, fought at a fountain the knight who had killed Sir Miles of the Glade – the same fountain, it may be supposed, at which Pellinore found the severed head in the adventure recounted above. The ambience is pagan, but is Giflet's title, 'the son of God', to be taken seriously? It seems rather that he was the son of a goddess, for behind Doon of Cardoel we can see a far more important figure, the goddess Don herself, whose sex seems in this instance to have been unaccountably transposed. The reason for making this equation is that the great pantheon of Welsh tradition known as 'the children of Don' includes Gilfaethwy. There is a striking correspondence between

GILFaEThwy son of DON
and GIFLET son of DOoN.

Having first been erected at this unidentified pagan site in Wales associated with the goddess Don, the table was moved to England, again by Merlin, and found its ultimate resting place at Camelot, the principal pagan site in the country and the place where the pagan king was crowned.

It is at first glance less easy to see pagan activities among the marvels associated with the table, because the first two to be drawn to our attention, the adventures of the white hart and of the white brachet, defy explanation. Even here, however, there is a slender link with paganism in the ritual associations of the actors and of parts of the action. Perhaps the hart and the brachet are expressions of some obscure form of cult symbolism, as suggested in R. Graves's *White Goddess* of the appearances in tradition of roebuck and dog. Whatever the case may have been in these two instances, other 'marvellous adventures' associated with the Round Table have the full flavour of paganism. A key example is the occasion of Galahad's assumption of his place in the perilous seat at the Round Table. On that festival of Pentecost, Arthur was reminded that by an old custom of the court he might not sit at meat before he had seen some adventure. The drawing of the sword followed. Pellinore's quest which started at Arthur's wedding feast, again before meat at the Round Table, is another action imbued with pagan motifs. The lady he set out to retrieve was that prime figure of native paganism, the Lady of the Lake, in her human personification of Nimue, who was the downfall of Merlin, and who accompanied Arthur in the ship that took him to Avilion. The knight who had siezed her was Sir Hontzlake, who (as Sir Ontzlake, Malory IV 12) belonged to that company distinguished as cult figures by being wounded through both thighs.

Other 'adventures' – strange occurrences for which, if we are to find an explanation, we must search in pagan custom – were met by chance in the field by members of the brotherhood. For instance, Sir Marhaus, Sir Gawaine and Sir

Uwaine, riding to find adventure, came at last (Malory IV 18)

into a great forest, that was named the country and forest of Arroy, and the country of strange adventures . . . and so they rode . . . and came [to] a fair fountain, and three damsels sitting thereby. . . . The eldest had a garland of gold about her head, and she was threescore winter of age or more, and her hair was white under the garland. The second damsel was of thirty winter of age, with a circlet of gold about her head. The third was but fifteen year of age, and a garland of flowers about her head.

The damsels explained that they were there for one purpose only, to lead errant knights towards strange adventures. Each of the three knights was to choose one of the damsels and to follow her directions. After a year they were to return to the fountain.

The analysis of paganism in chapters 1 to 3 provides several points of reference by which this episode can be recognized as of religious origin. It takes place at a 'fountain', most typical of cult sites. The fountain is in the forest of Arroy or Arbroie, that same adventurous forest of Diarwya in which Pwyll met his significant adventure, the name of which may be traced to the same root as Boia, identified with the head-in-well cult in St David's time. One of the participants is Uwaine who, as he is Morgan le Fay's son, is to be identified with the Owein we have already met as the 'knight of the fountain', and who is the son of King Uriens (possibly to be equated with Bran). There are three distinct lines of approach here – from the romances, the *Mabinogion* and the life story of a saint – each a link with paganism. So it is reasonable to look to paganism for an explanation of the three 'damsels' at the fountain. Presumably they represent the triplication of the goddess, and her three phases of virgin, mature woman and hag. Unfortunately the promised 'adventures', though by no means devoid of incidents attributable to pagan origins, do not give any grounds for suggesting differences in attitude or practice between the three phases.

When the knights of the Round Table are looked at as a body, it is at once apparent that some of the best known are cult figures, and that a substantial proportion of second-rank figures is made up of characters on the fringe of cult activity – the families of Ban, of Lot and of Pellinore, for instance. One important figure who does not fall into this grouping is Tristram, who appears to belong to a tradition parallel to the Arthurian mainstream. But in spite of his different background, there is a clue, though a slight one, to this hero's pagan status. It is that he fought a challenge on an island, and since an island is one of the characteristic sites of a ritual challenge, the incident should be examined to see if there are other correspondences to this pagan activity. What happened was that Tristram defeated Sir Marhaus, the son of King Marhalt of Ireland (or else the brother of the Queen of Ireland), who had challenged all comers to fight for the tribute of Cornwall, then outstanding seven years (Malory VIII 4). Marhaus has already been associated with paganism by his participation in the adventure of the three damsels. He is also described as the king's son of Ireland (Malory IV 17), a name sometimes suggestive of a pagan context.

Then there is the reward. The tribute of Cornwall for seven years sounds like kingship limited for the standard period of seven years; but Tristram is not remembered as enjoying this. He did, however, get the girl, Marhaus's niece (or sister) whom he loved but did not marry, like Launcelot with Elaine and Bors with Brangoire's daughter. Again like Launcelot and Bors and also Owein, Tristram needed special persuasion or assistance before the act of love was accomplished. In his case the agent was a love philtre which was administered, though unwittingly, by Dame Bragwaine.

In 'Bragwaine' there is a clue to the nature of the women who provide the hero with timely assistance, often of a supernatural kind, in this group of stories. In other stories in which the hero receives help in attaining his lady, the helper's name is Luned (*The Lady of the Fountain*), Linet (*Beaumains*), Elene (*Lybeaus*) or Helie (*Descouneus*). Bragwaine is presumably Bran-gwen or Branwen, Bran's sister – paralleled in the others by derivatives of the moon and the ever-present Elaine, but in each instance demoted from her true status as a goddess to little more than a handmaid.

It can be seen that enough of the basic structure of a cult-challenge has survived here for a guess to be made as to the originating circumstances. They would have been roughly as follows: The tribute of Cornwall, and its kingship (Marhaus with a hard ending is scarcely to be distinguished from Mark, the name of the king of Cornwall in this story), went to the successful contender in a challenge which took place at a cult site, an island, every seven years. The presiding deity was the goddess Branwen (who in Welsh tradition was married to the king of Ireland) and the priestess who became the victor's lover was described as the daughter of the goddess. No doubt in real life this system would have produced a future generation of heroes and heroines, as in the cases of Pellinore (with the Lady of the Rule), Bors and Launcelot; but there is no surviving trace of that having happened.

In any general review of the knights of the Round Table, first place must be given to Launcelot, and he, as it happens, has also occupied a prime position in this analysis of native paganism. After Launcelot, the next in importance is probably Gawaine and he, too, is clearly a pagan figure, as can be seen from the following brief account of his exploits. His father and mother were deities, his mother being either Malory's Morgawse – a paler shadow of her sister Morgan – or else possibly Geoffrey's Anna, another name of the goddess. He took part in the quest of the hart at the inauguration of the Round Table, and in the adventure of the three damsels at the fountain. His strength waxed and waned with the sun (Malory IV 18). The knights who overmatched him, Launcelot, Tristram, Bors, Percival, Pelleas and Marhaus (Malory IV 18), read like a roll-call of challenge knights. He attended a ceremonial in the Grail Castle which was followed by a night adventure in the perilous bed in which he was wounded in the shoulder by a flaming lance. He was driven away on the next day in the demeaning cart by an old woman with a scourge and pelted with filth, offal and old shoes. He had a son, Guiglain, who fought at a bridge, and he had two other sons by Brandiles's (i.e. Bran's) sister.

All in all, Gawaine, like Launcelot, Tristram, Percival, Bors and Galahad, has strong links with paganism. So has his brother, Gareth, who challenged the red knight of the glade by blowing a horn hung on a sycamore tree; in defeating him Gareth rescued Dame Lionesse of the Castle Perilous, from whose bed he was later disturbed and received a wound in the thigh by a gisarm. And yet another of the same 'family', the half-brother Mordred, bears the marks of a heroic birth: he was conceived in incest; his father was a king; he was destined to displace a higher power, his father; and an attempt was made to kill him while a child, by floating him to sea and leaving him to the mercy of wind and wave.

Some of the second-rank characters can be guessed to have a pagan origin solely on account of their parentage, such as Gaheris, the son of Lot, and Lamorak, the son of Pellinore. Others fit into this category by their behaviour as well, such as Uwaine the son of Uriens (Bran) and himself a challenger at a fountain; and Meliagaunce, the son of Bagdemagus (Bran), the half-brother of the damsel who threw a severed head into a well, and himself an abductor of Guenever. Sometimes the clue is heavily disguised, as in the case of the Questing Beast, followed by Sir Palamides the Saracen, which had 'a head like a serpent's head and a body like a leopard, buttocks like a lion, and footed like an hart; and in his body there was such a noise as it had been the noise of thirty couple of hounds questing'. This strange creature can only be guessed to have a pagan origin because it had originally been followed by Pellinore; but it is not Palamides's sole link with paganism, for he challenged Tristram to combat at a well and again at the 'peron and the grave beside Camelot' (Malory X 87).

Of the important knights of the Round Table, only one, Sir Kay, has so far gone unmentioned. But Kay is represented in the 'matter of Britain' as an inferior person, compared with his position in Welsh tradition as the foremost of Arthur's companions. It can scarcely be expected that this much reduced figure would provide any useful information about Kay's origin.

The Round Table was a table and also a symbol of the brotherhood of knights who 'belonged' to it. Either way it shows pagan associations – in the circumstances of its construction; in its original location at the seat of the goddess Don; in its perilous seat; as a focus of adventures; and in the association of all its major members with sacred kingship. The question now arises as to whether a mere structure of post-Roman times would have had the drawing power to attract so much pagan tradition. This argument can still be used of Arthur, who remains strangely aloof from the pagan cast which is acting out its various parts all around him, but can it be used of a table? Or are we to suppose that the table was part of the system which the great hero of the Celtic-speaking British attracted into his orbit, the focal point of the charmed circle of hero-knights and god-kings who together constitute a pagan pantheon? There is a description of the Round Table in the 'matter of Britain' which exactly fits an origin of this sort, but which would be extremely difficult to account for in any other way. It is as follows: in Uther's time all the knights had to be wounded in the face, but the custom of allowing a wounded knight to die at the Round Table fell into disuse when Launcelot, Galahad and Hector became companions, after which anyone sitting at a high feast had to have conquered a knight the previous week (Sommer V 130, 131).

This suggestion that the Round Table became a gathering of victorious challenge-knights corresponds to the conclusion that has just been arrived at, that the knights were cult figures, the majority being challenge-knights. It is also consistent with the behaviour of the pagan system in its implication of centralization, for its members must have been collected from a wide area. This matches the description of Camelot, the site of the Round Table, as being the principal pagan place in the country, and it matches the wide spread of locations from which the members come, including Orkney, Northumberland, North Wales, Cornwall and a number of unidentifiable kingdoms. The impression of centralization extends to the actions of the heroes. Typically, the knight 'errant' wanders in search of 'adventure' which turns out to be single combat in most cases. But one or two instances hint that this form of knightly conduct may have been evangelizing zeal, and its object to bring cult sites under the control of the Round Table.

Luned, for instance, in *The Lady of the Fountain*, offered to find a champion from Arthur's court, and her counterpart in another story, Linet, provides the 'adventure' necessary for Arthur's Pentecost court festival by requesting a knight to fight the Red Knight of the Glade for her lady, a task allotted to Gareth (Gawaine's brother) who succeeds, after a challenge by blowing a horn hanging from a sycamore tree, and later marries the lady, Dame Lionesse of the Castle Perilous, at Arthur's court.

The centralization inferred from tradition is perhaps a reflection of the same effect on the material plane. If the links between the cult activities we have been discussing and the floated and erected stones tend to locate these activities among the megalithic monuments of Salisbury Plain, that area has the same sort of central position in fact as the Arthurian court occupies in tradition.

In short, this new view of the Round Table corresponds in every way with the circumstances of pagan life which have already been observed. In addition, it appears to repeat a suggestion of sequence which we have already seen in the succession of maimed kings which preceded the assumption of kingship by Galahad. To give full effect to this latest revelation that wounded knights were habitually left to die there, we must redefine the Round Table as a central organization of ritually maimed ceremonial figures, which was in the course of time replaced by a national gathering of challenge-knights (including a contingent from Brittany). The gathering took place to honour a local representative of the Indo-European lightning god at a spring festival, at which an annual king was elected who would at the end of his term, like his sister, die a ritual death by bleeding into a sacred vessel for eucharistic consumption and be buried in a boat.

How does this redefinition of the Round Table affect our view of the position of Guenever, who is so closely linked to it? Not only was the table her dowry but she travelled with it to England and her wedding feast marked the commencement of the strange adventures of the Round Table. To this connection with the Round Table we must add that her father was a god, and that her name means 'White Phantom'[83] which could have a supernatural significance. In addition, she was abducted more than once, apparently, in one instance, with a view to being forcibly married to a pretender to the throne. This seems to mirror an aspect of paganism in which a national goddess provided 'sovereignty' by her marriage. And in Welsh tradition there are three Guenevers, suggesting the triple form in which the goddesses of the west so often appear. With these adumbrations of deity, there is a fair chance that Guenever was originally a goddess in Wales who, in some religious accommodation, also represented by the fetching of the Round Table from that country, extended her range, and that of the performance of her human representatives, to the national pagan centre on Salisbury Plain.

10 Merlin

The importance of the part played by Merlin in the affairs of the Round Table cannot be exaggerated. He suggested its manufacture to Uther; he supervised its construction; he arranged the marriage with which it came as a dowry; he organized its removal and (Malory III 5) he acted as a master of cermonies at it. And if we analyse this and Merlin's other actions it will be seen that, even without the episode of the Giants' Dance, his renown would still rest on a very firm footing. The difference is that in these other instances his powers were organizational rather than physical. He organized the great gathering on Salisbury Plain at which, apparently as a result of the presence of the forces of Ban and Bors (Sommer II 373 et seq), a truce was made with the rebel 'kings' (Sommer II 384), a substantial proportion of whom can be recognized as gods – Lot, Brangoire, Pelles and Pellinore. This sense of religious accommodation is repeated in the most important manifestation of the Round Table, the sense of common cause between cult figures of different types. The rebel kings (or their hero sons) turn up again as knights of the Round Table almost to a man (Malory XIX 11), and Pellinore was personally conducted by Merlin to his seat next to the Siege Perilous and the two seats reserved for the Annual King's immediate supporters. It looks very much as if tradition has preserved, by some fortunate chance, not only a reference to the moving of the bluestones but also a recollection of other aspects of the extraordinary skill, as an organizer, of the individual who moved them.

The status of the prime mover – whether the name Merlin belonged to a deity or a hero – cannot be determined, but of course the actual operator was a man or else a group or succession of men, of whom one was more than ordinarily gifted. He was, indeed, so much out of the ordinary that his fame persisted for 3000 years and the feat of transporting the stones still excites our imagination. If we take tradition at its face value, the following chain of events emerge as the background to the moving of the stones. Merlin was born in

Dyfed, the extreme south-west corner of what is now Wales. His supernatural parentage shows he was predestined to the religious sphere. He made his mark by organizing a standing conference of the maimed sacred kings of the surrounding localities at the headquarters of the cult of the goddess Don (also in what we now know as Wales), and a gruesome business it must have been, for they were allowed to die at their meeting-place. Don, we may guess from the scatter of forms of the name given to a bridge which was the focal point of a battle (Done, Dione, Diane, Dyanne), was none other than Diane, *la dieuesse del Bois* of the 'matter of Britain' – Diana of the Wood[84] – and so the patroness of the cult of the grove. Merlin himself was trained in astronomy and the practical aspects of megalithic construction, and he filled a formal ceremonial role as lover of a 'water-nymph' priestess. Because of his engineering skill, he was summoned to Logres as a consultant and took up his abode at a warm spring (possibly Bath), which was named after Galaphes, a maimed king and the builder of the Grail Castle. The cult belief was that Merlin represented lightning, and that his spouse was the goddess of the sacred grove and spring. He would in his official capacity have supposed himself able to control weather and would on occasion have worn a deerskin and antlers.

When his advice was sought on a suitable temple to enhance the national necropolis on Salisbury Plain, he proposed as a novel extension of the principle of religious accommodation he had practised at Cardoel that a temple should be removed bodily from his native Dyfed. In the event, one of the factions concerned, that of 'Ireland', resisted the move and it had to be carried through by force, the king of 'Ireland' being killed in the process. Merlin's answer to the general unrest which followed was to call a great gathering on Salisbury Plain, which was attended by contingents from all the factions involved. By getting the support of an alliance of two cults from Brittany, Merlin was able to organize a grand alliance. The religious confederation he had initiated in Wales was re-established on Salisbury Plain on an enlarged scale to include sects from all over Britain and even from across the Channel (but not from across the Irish Sea). The effect of Merlin's intervention in the religious history of this country was thus not merely to move the bluestones, but also to set up a climate of opinion which made the move desirable and to arrange the alliance which enabled the necessary manpower to be brought to bear on the project. As well as this, the element of centralization on Salisbury Plain which he encouraged was to lead in later years to the greater glories of the sarsen circle.

As a footnote to the affairs of Merlin, there are one or two lines of reasoning to be followed which, though they do not form part of the general argument of the book, perhaps have a certain amount of entertainment value.

It will have been noticed that the 'matter of Britain' tends to throw up more than one version of an original incident. There are several stories in which Merlin moves or floats stones, for instance, and the gathering on Salisbury Plain appears to be duplicated by a request by Merlin for more or less the same people to come to Camelot, a few pages later (Sommer II 414). It might well be the case that these, and that other notable removal by Merlin, the moving of the Round Table, are all fragments of the same original tradition. As it happens, there are a number of correspondences between the bluestone move and that of the Round Table, though whether they are to be taken seriously or not will depend on personal preference. They are as follows: The agent in each case was Merlin; the starting point was in Wales; the move took place by water and by land; the final resting place was Camelot; the king of Ireland met his death in an associated event. In addition, both the stone temple and the table are 'round', and both are tabular in form, in the sense that any flat stone on top of a vertical stone or stones is invariably called a table, as in the case of the Merchant's Table at Locmariaquer and the tavlas of the Balearics. It has even been argued that there is a general connection between the name 'round table' and circular Bronze Age monuments, there being one such stone circle actually called King Arthur's Round Table. Yet another lead in the same direction is provided by the explanation of the roundness of the Round Table in the 'matter of Britain'. It is not the familiar medieval explanation that it was round so that no one sitting at the table had precedence over any other. This was not true of the original Round Table because that did have a high seat, the siege perilous, from which, as we saw in the election of

Pellinore, precedence was counted. No, the true reason was astronomical and to do with the 'circumstances of the planets and the stars', which sounds like a recollection of the recently noticed astronomical-observatory aspect of Stonehenge.[85]

If these correspondences carry conviction, then the events detailed in the last few pages can easily be condensed into a single composite picture, and the cult pattern attached to the Round Table can be imagined as taking place at Stonehenge itself. If not, then the two strands of tradition remain close in space and time, and each is firmly linked to the same scheme of sacred kingship. The picture is not very different, just a little more diffuse, as is appropriate to a tradition of such extreme age.

11 Arthur

One last topic now remains to be discussed. That is the relationship of King Arthur to the pagan scene that has been unfolded. It has been shown that nearly all his kindred, his subjects and their major activities have nothing to do with the Christian king of the fifth to sixth centuries A D. The list so far of individuals and actions closely linked with Arthur but having an origin in pagan cults is, briefly, as follows:

His father and his begetting.

His mother's daughters.

His mentor, Merlin.

His accession to the throne as a result of drawing the sword from the stone.

His part in the contests between deities which marked the establishment of his authority.

His marriage.

The Round Table and its associated adventures.

His adversaries (and later his allies): Lot, Uriens and Pellinore.

His allies: Ban and Bors, and Balin and Balan.

His principal subjects (largely children of the above):
Gawaine, Gareth, Owein, Percival, Launcelot, Bors, Galahad, Tristram and Marhaus.

and their ladies:
Brandiles's sister, the Lady of the Castle Perilous, the Lady of the Fountain, Pelles's daughter, Brangoire's daughter, the queen of Ireland's daughter.

The 'adventures' which characterize his reign:
combats at fountain and ford, tournaments fought for a lady's love, quests and night adventures.

And to these, now we approach the end of his story, are to be added:

His defeat and mortal wound at the very place where Merlin had called the great gathering on Salisbury Plain.

The episode of the sword thrown into the lake, where it was caught by a mysterious hand. This is clearly an offering to the spirit of the waters, an exact parallel to the treasures thrown into sacred waters in pagan times.

The enigmatic ending to his earthly life, when he was carried away to Avilion accompanied by his goddess-sister Morgan le Fay, by the queen of the Waste Land and by the chief lady of the lake. A departure to an island paradise reminiscent (like the deaths of Percival's sister and the Lady of Shalott) of boat burial.

The list is an impressive one but it is irrelevant to whether there was or was not a historical Arthur. That is a question which can only be decided by enquiry into the circumstances of the post-Roman period, and since this analysis of the 'matter of Britain' has shown that its components are almost without exception associated with an earlier paganism, they obviously have no bearing on the history of the fifth and sixth centuries A D. The effect of this analysis is, it is true, to strip from the historical figure what are, in the context of his period, no more than romantic improbabilities, but he is left with a renown sufficient to attract into his train a complete mythology, and to finish up with a pantheon as his attendants. No mean feat in an era from which few names are remembered. The interest of the list is therefore primarily the light it sheds on Arthur's shadowy precursor, whose image has been cast onto the background of the post-Roman scene with a vividness which far surpasses that of the few human figures who can be discerned. What do we now know of this proto-Arthur or prehistorical Arthur? Was he a god, or a hero, or was he a mere secular ruler?

Unfortunately there is no clear answer to these questions. The main difficulty is that 'Arthur' himself stays very much in the background. His principal characteristic is not performance but position. He is a central figure whose battles and alliances are not with mortal men but with pagan deities. We need not, therefore, be surprised that he does not easily fall into any of the categories we have been discussing, for he is in a class by himself, the organizer of an alliance among deities, the head of a pantheon of his own making. His is the name which represents the coalition of deities which took over the pre-existing national cult centre on Salisbury Plain at the beginning of the Bronze Age, a coalition which resulted from the same forces as were responsible for the bluestone move. We can tell this because the agents and accessories of Arthur's ascent to power – Merlin, Balin, the lightning symbol (Balin's sword = Excalibur), the death of the king of 'Ireland' (Arthur killed Rions, king of Ireland, in single combat and also captured from him a shining sword of the same style as Excalibur), and the setting (the floating stone and the peron were both near Camelot) – are exactly those which have already been shown to be associated with the bluestone move. 'Arthur' is also the name which represents the centralized and expanding religious system exemplified by the Round Table, and the defeat and departure of 'Arthur' the break-up of the system. The time-scale of these events need not be thought of as restricted to a single life-span, for the 'Arthur' we now have before us is not a man but a coalition of deities, his 'reign' the period of supremacy of that coalition, and his 'court' the constituent deities or, on a human scale, the men and women who gathered at Stonehenge to represent the natures of their local deities by ritual acts. This coalition could have lasted for centuries. We must suppose that it at least covered the brilliant period of the sarsen circle and the Wessex culture (in which burials were sometimes made in canoe-like hollowed-out tree-trunk coffins), since the 'Arthurian' tradition has not been overlaid by any other. But this line of argument should probably be carried even further. That the tradition has survived at all suggests that it was part of a corpus of thought which still had meaning and validity, though probably in a debased form, until comparatively late in pre-Christian times.

Our post-Frazer visit to Camelot has produced some interesting and unexpected conclusions, but none more so than this final suggestion that 'Arthur's' sphere of influence was the Bronze Age. The route that has been followed to this end is one of detailed consideration of numerous traces of paganism in traditional stories. It is the minutiae alone that have so far been considered. How does this conclusion stand when it is viewed against the general background of pre-history? For it to be acceptable, a certain set of circumstances must have obtained. We must suppose that the last considerable religious impetus before Christianity (apart from the short-lived introductions of Roman troops) coincided with the arrival of Indo-Europeans; that this system declined into, rather than being replaced by, its successors (at least in some perhaps limited area); and that (again probably in a restricted situation) the activities of the founding fathers became incorporated in some canon comparable to the Old

Testament in its capacity to survive. These necessary circumstances are all within the bounds of possibility. And the final conclusion outlined above fits the likely original situation in several other ways. It caters for an accommodation with the pre-Indo-European system and for a substantial modification on the arrival of people calling themselves Celts (or Galli). And it is difficult to think of any other period which could give rise to legends of a 'king' with a more than insular importance, and which could give rise to legends of a more than southern British spread. Above all, what other period in British prehistory had the brilliance and power to provide for local 'heroes' a setting to compare – however much ruder and more archaic it may have been – with Homer's Mycenae?

For just as the Greek tradition refers to real men not, as was at one time thought, of the Iron Age, but of a more brilliant Bronze Age, so does Britain's 'Arthurian' tradition. Through the inconsistencies and irrationalities of an imperfect medium of transmission there are occasional flashes of clarity. The confederation of Mycenaean princes which destroyed Troy is paralleled by the great gathering on Salisbury Plain which settled the power structure that provided the labour force to build Britain's most magnificent prehistoric monument, and the doings of the heroes of Homer are paralleled by those of Malory, but with a difference. The acts of the British heroes and heroines (including the British Helen) were generally of ritual significance. Nevertheless, the stories of personal combat and love and death and birth are accounts of the actions of real men and real women, the men and women who inspired the toiling throngs engaged in the construction of great sarsen structures and who, in doing so, created a tradition which, like the stones themselves, has survived the passing of millennia. Though the tradition was long-lasting, its meaning was forgotten many centuries ago, as, indeed, was the significance of the stones. But by a fortunate chance we can still discern the residue of a Bronze-Age oral 'literature' in the tales which cluster around pagan Camelot and its ruler, that original Arthur so aptly described by Tennyson as the

> . . . gray king whose name, a ghost,
> Streams like a cloud, man-shaped, from mountain peak,
> And cleaves to cairn and cromlech still.

APPENDIX I

A possible correspondence between a traditional story of 'invasion' and archaeological fact

Although it is extremely difficult to match the partial view of an event in the distant past, as seen through the distortions and filters of a traditional story, with the material remains of the same event available to archaeologists, a conjecture can be made in the case of Joseph of Arimathea. Tradition records entry from abroad and (under a veneer of Christianity) the sinister symbolism of the cup of blood, the ritual of the fish-meal, the large-scale conversion of the inhabitants of the previous holy cities (which have been linked, by their association with the bluestone move, to Salisbury Plain), and the replacement of their principal temple by a church of St Stephen. Unlike some invasion myths with their name-giving 'founding father', this does not sound like a fiction to explain the existence of a tribe or people, and the supporting cast is associated with paganism with a consistency which suggests a genuine tradition. So we may have identified a record, however imperfect, of an invasion and its consequences; but how is it possible even to consider matching this with the archaeological evidence of the original event, when, looking backward through the layered earth, we see so many different styles of living and of disposing of the dead? Since the source of our information is native paganism, we can a once discount the post-Roman Germanic and Scandinavian invasions, and the Roman occupation itself. But before that there seems plenty to choose from. The latest foreign influence, in the last century before the Roman occupation, was Belgic, and emanated from the opposite shores of the Channel. Before that the style of the La Tène culture was imprinted on native artifacts; before La Tène there was some Hallstatt influence; before Hallstatt there was Urnfield; before Urnfield, Wessex; and before Wessex the Beaker culture predominated, with various admixtures of other cultures from the steppes. Prior even to that, the first-farmers acknowledged various overseas influences in their styles of burial, and, of course, owed their own agricultural techniques to developments in the Middle East. Where, in this long list, are we to begin?

The answer to this question lies in the nature of the stimuli which produced the changes from stage to stage in this long cultural evolution. In all the instances listed, the number of arrivals into Britain has always been small or neglible. There has never been any displacement of the original inhabitants on a substantial scale. Even in the Anglo-Saxon invasion, with its complete replacement of the original Celtic speech, the invaders are now thought to have numbered only about ten percent of the population of lowland Britain. So the native British are likely to have made a substantial contribution of genetic material to subsequent 'Englishness', and probably a considerable cultural contribution too. When we examine the prehistoric period, we shall find far less evidence of displacement. The seeds of change will be found to have germinated in the native soil of earlier cultures, and the field, for comparison with Joseph's adventures, can be very much reduced.

Starting with the *Belgae*, this movement, besides being local only to Kent, 'need not', according to Ashbee,[86] 'have involved great numbers of people who would have wrought widespread changes in the manners and customs of the indigenes, the *Cantii*'.

Iron Age features, including specific ceramic traditions, have their roots in the Middle Bronze Age, and, again according to Ashbee,[87] 'provide a pattern of continuity to the threshold of Roman times'. Apart from the *Belgae*, only two intrusive elements can be seen. The earlier of these, the Hallstatt sword burial from Ebberston in Yorkshire, 'scarcely indicates a major influx' and the later, the migration of the *Parisi* from Gaul to the Yorkshire Wolds, was extremely local.

The same emphasis on continuity and the overwhelming contribution of native elements is to be found at the next previous cultural change. Ashbee's opinion is that it is 'unnecessary to invoke continental urnfields as a source and inspiration for the cremation cemetery mode of burial. The cremation cemeteries and the urns have an origin in later Neolithic cremation cemeteries and pottery of the Grooved Ware variety'.[88]

That most distinctive and most dominating of British native

cultures, the Wessex culture, is the next to come under review. The heroic-warrior style of the earlier Beaker incursions, now assimilated into the indigenous societies, was matched by that of equally aggrandized aboriginals. The radical nature of the new culture is no longer thought of as due to external stimulus and ethnic movement. Instead, stress is placed on the contribution of the mixed indigenous tradition.[89]

It is not until we come to the Beaker incursions that we find the latest occasion, prior to the Roman occupation, when external stimulus had a profound effect. Their success may have been due to force of arms, or ideology, or bronze technology. However it was achieved, the 'initial Beaker influx must have come to terms with the later Neolithic communities. The subsequent social amalgam, already with its warrior element, led to the later political dominance of Wessex by the Stonehenge-based community'[90] and ultimately to 'the political domination of Britain from Wessex'.[91]

Here at last there is a substantial enough discontinuity in cultural pattern to compare with the story of Joseph. Looking at the details, it is at once evident that there is a coincidence of place, for, just like the Beaker-folk, Joseph at once set about 'converting' the Sarrasen inhabitants of 'Sarisberie' Plain; there is a coincidence in time, for the affair of the floated stones takes the legendary scene back to the beginning of the Bronze Age; and there is a coincidence of symbol, a cup in each case. As well as these coincidences, the result in each case was compromise – Joseph married the daughter of the king of the Sarrasens – and federation, and the instrument of unification in each case was round and flat – for the Beaker-folk, the henge,[92] and for Joseph's successors, the Round Table.

There are still more reasons for supposing we may have a match between the affairs of the 'matter of Britain' and the Late Neolithic/Beaker accommodation. One is the scale. It is difficult to imagine any later occasion on which a cultural province embracing, according to the literary sources, a place as distant as Orkney (whose sacred hierarachy formed an important element of the Arthurian confederation), could be matched with an archaeological province of the same wide extent. (The styles of artefact found in Orkney match those of southern Britain.) Another reason is the fundamental nature of the changes which seem to have taken place at that time: a change from collectivism to individualism; a change from belief in a mother goddess to belief in a pantheon in which gods were prominent; a change to a warrior-dominated society; and probably the introduction of an Indo-European language.[93] The impact of these fundamental shifts, added to the overpowering grandeur of the religious buildings of the period, explain why this particular era made an indelible mark on the collective memory.

The view outlined above of the relationship between 'invasion' and cultural change not only suggests how the pagan substratum of the 'matter of Britain' arose, but also emphasizes the continuity which was necessary for survival. This degree of continuity finds archaeological backing in the archaic characteristics of some hill-forts, and their siting over and around Neolithic causewayed enclosures. Features which 'may be connected with the renaissance of early rites'[94] have apparently survived into Iron Age times.

Archaeology and tradition appear to coincide in describing the pre-Christian religion of Britain to be the result of an accommodation at the beginning of the Bronze Age between indigenous and introduced cults, an amalgam which appears never to have been superseded. The native paganism of the last two millennia BC thus inherited, and perpetuated, elements from a still earlier era. One such is annual kingship, which was probably introduced with cereal crops, and was still associated with Joseph's successors in fully Celtic times. And the title Fisher King or Rich Fisher sounds like a survival from a period when agricultural produce was not the main source of sustenance.

Other possible correspondences between tradition and archaeology

The Cornish Fogou

The Norse *Tristramssaga*, completed in 1226, translates the text of a lost French Tristan romance. It is believed to reproduce the original accurately. In it, the sanctuary of the lovers Tristram and Iseult, after they had left Mark's court, is described as follows:

They found a secret place beside a certain water, and in the hillside, that heathen men let hew and adorn in olden time with mickle skill and fair craft, and this was all vaulted and the entrance digged deep in the ground, and there was a secret way in running along below ground. Over the house lay much earth and thereon stood the fairest tree upon the hillside.[95]

This description of a man-made underground chamber calls to mind the type of construction known in Cornwall as a *fogou*. This kind of structure generally consists of an underground passage with walled sides and a slab roof, with more than one entrance and one or more low and narrow side passages leading nowhere. S. C. Harris[96] sees four points of correspondence between the passage quoted above and a particular fogou at St Euny near Land's End, which is unusual in Britain in having access to a round corbelled chamber. They are:

'all vaulted'	the corbelled chamber?
'the entrance digged deep in the ground'	the creep-hole entrance?
'a secret way in running along below ground'	the long main passage?
'over the house lay much earth'	the fogou had been earthed over

The purpose for which fogous were built is not known. It is suspected that they may have had 'more than a purely utilitarian function',[97] though cult objects are lacking in all the examples excavated. The suggestion that the fogou under consideration may have had some religious use is reinforced by the presence in the immediate vicinity of a holy well, dedicated to St Euny but also known as the giant's well; by the close presence of several features named after Bran; and by the presence in the literary account of the significant single tree.

Patricia M. L. Christie tentatively assigns the construction of the corbelled chamber of this particular fogou to the fifth century BC, and radio-carbon dating gives a median date in the second century BC for an item found in the debris on the floor of the passage.[98]

Branwen's Grave

When, in the *Mabinogion*, Bran's head had been struck off, the first place that the seven survivors of the battle with Ireland came to was Anglesey. They carried the head, and Branwen, Bran's sister, accompanied them. After they had landed at Aber Alaw,

they sat down and rested them. Then she looked on Ireland and the Island of the Mighty, what she might see of them. 'Alas, Son of God,' said she, 'woe is me that ever I was born: two good islands have been laid waste because of me!' And she heaved a great sigh, and with that broke her heart. And a four sided grave was made for her, and she was buried there on the bank of the Alaw.[99]

The story was taken up a great deal later, when a farmer, looking for stone in 1813 at a place called Ynys Bronwen, dug into a barrow and found 'a cist formed of coarse flags canted and covered over. On removing the lid, he found it contained an urn placed with its mouth downwards, full of ashes and half-calcined fragments of bone.'[100]

There are three correspondences here:

The name of the river, Alaw.

The name Branwen (the slight difference in spelling does not suggest to commentators that there were two different people, but there is some doubt as to which was the original form).

The four-sided grave may, somewhat inconclusively, be supposed to correspond to the small chamber of flagstones in which the urn was found.

When the discovery was made, it was inferred from these correspondences that the ashes in the urn were Branwen's. Though whether the same conclusion would have been reached if it had been realized at that time that the burial was Bronze Age, about 1400 BC, it is now impossible to say.

More recently the site has been professionally excavated by Frances Lynch. Her findings are reported in the *Transactions of the Anglesey Antiquarian Society*, 1966.[101] The burial was multiple, and two or three of the urns with burnt bones in them were accompanied by pots of dark earth mixed with charcoal which looked as if scraped up from the ashes of the funeral pyre. Except for earth and charcoal, there were only two fragments of bone in each pot (though in one pot, which was broken, only one piece of bone was found). One of the urns which had an accompanying pot of soil was evidently of greater importance, for it was enclosed in a rough cist of flags barely big enough to hold the urn. This urn contained a necklace of beads of jet, amber and bone, an article of considerable rarity and value, with no equivalent in Wales.

The presence of the cist, the style of the urns found, and the nature of the disturbance all support the accuracy of the report of the 1813 discovery, but they add nothing to the short list of correspondences, except, perhaps, in one macabre detail. The fragments of bone in the accompanying pots were pairs of ear-bones from new-born babies. It looks as if a child sacrifice was associated with the burial of each urn.

Needless to say, there is nothing in tradition which refers directly to the ritual death of children. Only two incidents come to mind in which a child dies in circumstances which suggest that they are eroded versions of such an original. In one, Branwen's son, Gwern, had the kingship of Ireland conferred upon him. He was then thrust headfirst into a blazing fire by his uncle.[102] In the other, King Gurguran, whose son had been killed by a giant, had the body cooked and divided among all his people to be eaten.[103] We do not know whom Gurguran might correspond to in Welsh legend, but his name looks as if it might be a version of Gocuran (alternatively Ogrfran or Ogfran), a compound which contains the name Bran, grammatically modified, in the element -fran or -uran.

There is no reference to burial in either of these episodes, but in the context of sacred kingship, to which these figures belong, the violent death of royal personages may be supposed to have a ritual implication. This inference is strongly supported in the case of Gurguran's son by the general distribution and eating of the cooked flesh, which can scarcely bear any other interpretation. So, to set against the archaeological evidence suggestive of child sacrifice, there is a tradition of the ritual killing of children; to which it may be added that the remains of the real child in 'Branwen's Grave' were found in what appears to be the debris of a fire, which could be a parallel to the mode of death (according to tradition) of Branwen's child.

St Carannog's Altar

The first reference to the Round Table was made by Wace, a Norman, after Geoffrey of Monmouth's *Historia* was published but before the first flowering of the 'matter of Britain' at the hands of Chrétien de Troyes and Thomas, the author of *Tristan*. But there is an earlier episode in which Arthur is associated with a table. About 1100, a life of the Welsh saint, Carannog, describes how the saint floated an altar on the Severn, for a divine guide to his landing.[104] It floated to the realm of Cato and Arthur, apparently joint rulers, who were living in a place called Dindraithov. Arthur would have liked to make a table of it, but its usefulness for this purpose was restricted by certain magical properties.

Susan Kelly has suggested that this association between Arthur and a table might be a garbled reference to the Round Table.[105] It is perhaps also worth commenting that to have 'floated on the Severn' is what would be expected of a recollection of the moving of the bluestones. So, if the alternative explanation, given in *The Real Camelot*, of the reality underlying the Round Table is correct, the altar floated on the Severn could be a distant ripple from the floating of a real stone.

Notes on the text

Authors and titles are given in full in the Bibliography

1 *Arthur's Britain* 163
2 *The Nature of Greek Myths* 278
3 *Historia Regum Britanniae* VIII, 10
4 *Stonehenge* 215
5 *Antiquity* XV, 60, 308
6 *The Mabinogion* 55
7 *Totem and Taboo* 79
8 *ibid.* 84
9 *The Mabinogion* 55
10 *ibid.* 6
11 'la plus rice cite que li sarrasin eussent en la grant bartaigne. & estoit de si grant auctorite que li roi paien i estoit corone. & i estoit la mahoumerie plus grant & plus haute quen nule autre cyte qui el roialme fust' (*Sommer* I 24)
12 *The Golden Bough* 1 ff.
13 *The Mabinogion* 158ff.
14 (a) to (f) are from Luttrell, *The Creation of the First Arthurian Romance* 99, 99, 248, 217, 124 and 218.
15 U. von Zatzikhoven, *Lanzelet* VIII, quoted by Paton
16 *The Golden Bough* 274ff.
17 *Sir Lancelot of the Lake* (tr. Paton)
18 Tr. S. Evans I 200
19 *Folklore* 48 (1937) 263
20 *The Golden Bough* 327
21 *ibid.* 329
22 *The High History of the Holy Grail* (tr. S. Evans) I 164

23 *ibid.* II 79
24 Newstead, *Bran the Blessed in Arthurian Romance* 172
25 *The Mabinogion* 17
26 Ross, *Pagan Celtic Britain* 288
27 *The Golden Bough* 350
28 Loomis, *Wales and the Arthurian Legend* 47
29 See my text, p. 118
30 Loomis, *Arthurian Tradition and Chrétien de Troyes* 28
31 Rhys, *Studies in the Arthurian Legend* 142
32 Tacitus, *Germania* (Loeb edition) 321
33 Rees and Rees, *Celtic Heritage* 233ff.
34 *Parzival* (tr. Zeydel and Morgan) lines 701–3
35 Newstead, *Bran the Blessed in Arthurian Romance* 81–2
36 *The Mabinogion* 129
37 Bromwich, in *Arthurian Literature in the Middle Ages* (ed. Loomis) 50
38 The wide scatter of 'Bel-' names in Pagan contexts from India to Ireland has been commented on by Rees and Rees, *Celtic Heritage* 365
39 The closeness of the insular forms Balin and Belinus to the Continental Belenus (popular in Roman times) could indicate a more basic relationship.
40 *Celtic Myth and Legend* 356
41 Loomis, *Wales and the Arthurian Legend* 105

42 *ibid.* 135
43 *ibid.* 118
44 *ibid.* 118
45 *ibid.* 118
46 *ibid.* 119
47 *ibid.* 114
48 *The Golden Bough* 164
49 Ross, *Pagan Celtic Britain* 228
50 Geoffrey of Monmouth, *History of the Kings of Britain* II 14
51 *The Evolution of the Grail Legend* 39
52 *Pagan Celtic Britain* 94
53 Graves, *The White Goddess* 283–4
54 *Antiquaries Journal* III (1923) 239f.
55 Atkinson, *Stonehenge* 214
56 *Concise Oxford Dictionary of Place Names* (4th ed.)
57 *Legendary History and Folklore of Stonehenge* 11
58 *Prehistoric Britain* 59
59 *Celtic Heritage* 41
60 *ibid.* 16
61 *ibid.* 365
62 Ashbee, *The Ancient British* 203
63 See note 11.
64 *Arthur's Britain* 163
65 Loomis, *Celtic Myth and Arthurian Romance* 190
66 Newstead, *Bran the Blessed in Arthurian Romance* 145
67 Rees and Rees, *Celtic Heritage* 53
68 Ross, *Pagan Celtic Britain* 221
69 Chadwick, *The Celts* 50
70 *The Ancient British* 43
71 Ross, *Pagan Celtic Britain* 34
72 p. 223
73 *ibid.* 226
74 *ibid.* 222
75 *ibid.* 227

76 *ibid.* 227
77 Rhys, *Studies in the Arthurian Legend* 239
78 'toutes les choses si degastes comme se effoudres fust courus en chascun lieu' (Legge 81)
79 'avoit le uiare si ardent comme foudre' (Sommer I 77)
80 p. 356
81 Rhys, *Studies in the Arthurian Legend* 162
82 and also Lambar, Lambart, Labain and Labran
83 Bromwich, *Trioedd Ynys Prydein* 380–1
84 'Del bois' applied to Diana is matched by the title 'forester' given to Doon of Cardoel. Since, according to Frazer, Diana has a consort Dianus, it is perhaps this male deity who has been remembered in association with Cardoel. If so, Gilfaethwy would be the son of the British equivalents to Diana and Dianus – Don (Done, Dione, etc.) and Dyonas.
  In the 'matter of Britain', Dyonas is referred to as the son of Diane dieuesse del bois and as the father of the damsel of the lake variously known as Elaine, Nimue and Vivienne. Welsh tradition hints at Beli as a possible consort for Don.
85 'en ce quele est apelee table roonde est entendu la rondece (lauironment) del monde & la chertainites (la circonstance) des planetes . . . & el firmament par quoi len voit les etoiles & les autres choses dont len ne poet pas dire' (Sommer VI 55)
86 *The Ancient British* 220
87 *ibid.* 42
88 *ibid.* 42

89 *ibid.* 160	**98** *ibid.* 331
90 *ibid.* 40	**99** *The Mabinogion* 38
91 *ibid.* 47	**100** Fenton, *Cambro-Briton*,
92 *ibid.* 137	1820 [ii] 71
93 *ibid.* 133	**101** *Transactions of the Anglesey*
94 *ibid.* 203	*Antiquarian Society*, 1966, 1
95 S. C. Harris, *Romania* (98)	**102** *The Mabinogion* 36
316	**103** *Perlesvaus* branch 5
96 *ibid.* 318	**104** Chambers, *Arthur of Britain*
97 Patricia M. L. Christie, *Proc.*	82
Prehistoric Society (44) 332	**105** *Folklore* (87) 223

Bibliography

ALCOCK, L. *'By South Cadbury is that Camelot . . .' Excavations at Cadbury Castle 1966–1970*, London/New York, 1972.
—— *Arthur's Britain*, Harmondsworth, 1971.
ASHBEE, P. *The Bronze Age Round Barrow in Britain*, London, 1960.
—— *The Ancient British*, Norwich, 1978.
ASHE, G. *King Arthur's Avalon*, London & Glasgow, 1957.
ASHE, G. and others *The Quest for Arthur's Britain*, London, 1968.
ATKINSON, R. J. C. *Stonehenge*, Harmondsworth, 1979.
BARBER, R. *The Figure of Arthur*, London, 1972.
—— *King Arthur in legend and history*, Ipswich, 1973.
BRADLEY, R. *The Prehistoric Settlement of Britain*, London/Boston, 1978.
BRANSTON, B. *Gods of the North*, London/New York, 1980.
BRIGGS, K. M. *Fairies in Tradition and Literature*, London, 1967.
BROHOLM, H. S. and HALD, M. *Costumes of the Bronze Age in Denmark*, London, 1940.
BROMWICH, R. *Trioedd Ynys Prydein*, Cardiff, 1961.
BRYANT, N. (tr.) *The High Book of the Grail*, Cambridge/Totowa, N.J., 1978.
BURL, A. *The Stone Circles of the British Isles*, New Haven/London, 1976.
CERAM, C. W. *Gods, Graves and Scholars*, London/New York, 1952.
CHADWICK, NORA *The Druids*, Cardiff, 1966.
—— *The Celts*, Harmondsworth, 1972.
CHAMBERS, E. K. *Arthur of Britain*, London, 1927.
CHILDE, V. G. *The Prehistory of Scotland*, London, 1935.

CLARK, J. G. D. *Archaeology and Society*, London, 1968.
—— *World Prehistory – an Outline*, Cambridge, 1961.
CLARK, J. G. D. and PIGGOTT, S. *Prehistoric Societies*, London, 1965.
CLARKE, D. L. *Analytical Archaeology*, London, 1968.
CUNLIFFE, B. W. *Iron Age Communities in Britain*, London/Boston, 1974.
CURTIS, E. *History of Ireland*, London, 1950.
DAMES, M. *The Silbury Treasure*, London/New York, 1976.
DANIEL, G. E. and O'RIORDAIN, S. P. *New Grange and the Bend of the Boyne*, London, 1964.
DANIEL, G. E. (ed.) *Myth or Legend?* London, 1955.
DAVIDSON, H. R. E. *Scandinavian Mythology*, London, 1969.
EKWALL, E. *Concise Dictionary of English Place-Names*, Oxford, 1960.
EVANS, E. E. *The Personality of Ireland*, Cambridge, 1973.
EVANS, S. (tr.) *The High History of the Holy Grail*, London, 1898.
FARNELL, L. R. *Outline History of Greek Religion*, London, 1920.
FENTON, RICHARD 'Tomb of Bronwen' (An account of excavations at Yns Bronwen, communicated by Sir R. Colt Hoare), *The Cambro-Briton and General Celtic Repository*, London, Oct. 1820, 71–3.
FOSTER, I. Ll. and DANIEL, G. E. (ed.) *Prehistoric and Early Wales*, London, 1965.
FOX, C. *Life and Death in the Bronze Age*, London, 1959.
FRAZER, SIR J. G. *The Golden Bough* (abridged ed.), London, 1949.
—— *Adonis*, London, 1932.
FREUD, S. *Totem and Taboo*, Harmondsworth, 1938.
GARSTANG, J. *The Land of the Hittites*, Liverpool, 1910.
GEIPEL, J. *The Europeans. An Ethnohistorical Survey*, London, 1969.
GELLING, M. *Signposts to the Past*, London, Melbourne and Toronto, 1978.
GELLING, P. and DAVIDSON, H. E. *The Chariot of the Sun*, London, 1969.
GEOFFREY OF MONMOUTH *History of the Kings of Britain* (tr. S. Evans), London, 1966.
GILDAS and NENNIUS (tr. J. A. Giles), London, 1841.
GLOB, P. V. *The Bog People*, London, 1969.
GRAVES, R. *The White Goddess*, London, 1948.
—— *The Greek Myths*, Harmondsworth, 1966.
GREEN, C. P. 'Pleistocene River Gravels and the Stonehenge Problem', *Nature* 243 (London, 1973), 214.
GRINSELL, L. V. *Legendary history and folklore of Stonehenge*, St Peter Port, 1975.
GRUFFYDD, W. J. *Folklore and Myth in the Mabinogion*, Cardiff, 1958.
HARRIS, S. C. 'The Cave of Lovers in the "Tristramssaga" and related Tristan romances', *Romania* 98 (Paris, 1977), 306–30, 460–500.
HAWKES, J. *Dawn of the Gods*, London, 1968.
HAWKES, J. and C. *Prehistoric Britain*, London, 1949.
HULL, E. *Folklore of the British Isles*, London, 1928.

JACKSON, K. H. *A Celtic Miscellany*, London, 1951.
—— *The Gododdin*, Edinburgh, 1969.
JAMES, E. O. *The Ancient Gods*, London, 1960.
—— *Sacrifice and Sacrament*, London, 1962.
JARMAN, A. O. H. *The Legend of Merlin*, Cardiff, 1960.
JONES, F. *The Holy Wells of Wales*, Cardiff, 1954.
JONES, G. and JONES, T. (tr.) *The Mabinogion*, London/New York, 1949.
JONES, W. B. T. and FREEMAN, E. A. *The History and Antiquities of St David's*, London, 1856.
JONES, W. L. *King Arthur in History and Legend*, Cambridge, 1911.
JUNG, E. and VON FRANZ, M. L. *The Grail Legend*, London, 1971.
KELLAWAY, G. A. 'Glaciation and the Stones of Stonehenge', *Nature* 233 (London, 1971), 30–5.
KENDRICK, SIR T. D. *The Druids*, London, 1927.
KIRK, G. S. *The Nature of Greek Myths*, Harmondsworth, 1974.
KITTO, H. D. F. *The Greeks*, Harmondsworth, 1957.
KRAPPE, H. A. *The Science of Folklore*, London, 1961.
LEGGE, M. D. *Le Roman de Balain*, Manchester, 1942.
LOOMIS, R. S. *Celtic Myth and Arthurian Romance*, New York, 1927.
—— *Arthurian Tradition and Chrétien de Troyes*, New York, 1949.
—— *Wales and the Arthurian Legend*, Cardiff, 1956.
—— *The Grail. From Celtic Myth to Christian Symbol*, New York, 1963.
LOOMIS, R. S. (ed.) *Arthurian Literature in the Middle Ages*, Oxford, 1959.
LUMIANSKY, R. M. (ed.) *Malory's Originality. A critical study of Le Morte Darthur*, Baltimore, 1964.
LUTTRELL, C. *The Creation of the First Arthurian Romance. A Quest*, London, 1974.
MACALISTER, R. A. S. *Tara. A pagan sanctuary of Ancient Ireland*, London, 1931.
MARKALE, J. *Les Celtes et la civilisation celtique: mythe et histoire*, Paris, 1969.
MacCULLOCH, J. A. *Religion of the Ancient Celts*, Edinburgh, 1911.
MacKIE, E. *The Megalith Builders*, Oxford, 1977.
MALORY, SIR T. *Le Morte Darthur*. First printed 1485 (edition used: Medici, London, 1911, reprinted 1935).
MATARASSO, P. M. (tr.) *The Quest of the Holy Grail*, Harmondsworth, 1969.
NENNIUS — *see* GILDAS.
NEWSTEAD, H. *Bran the Blessed in Arthurian Romance*, New York, 1939.
NILSSON, N. M. P. *Greek Popular Religion*, New York, 1940.
—— *History of Greek Religion*, Oxford, 1949.
O'RAHILLY, T. F. *Early Irish History and Mythology*, Dublin, 1946.
OWEN, D. D. R. *The Evolution of the Grail Legend*, London/Edinburgh, 1968.

PAGE, D. *History and the Homeric Iliad*, Berkeley/Los Angeles, 1972.
PARKE, H. W. *Greek Oracles*, London, 1967.
PATON, L. A. (tr.) *Sir Lancelot of the Lake*, London, 1929.
PEI, M. *The Families of Words*, New York, 1962.
PIGGOTT, S. 'The Sources of Geoffrey of Monmouth', *Antiquity* XV (1941), 305–19.
—— *Neolithic Cultures of the British Isles*, Cambridge, 1954.
—— *The Druids*, London/New York, 1968.
POLLARD, J. *Helen of Troy*, London, 1965.
POWELL, T. G. E. *The Celts*, London/New York, 1980.
REES, A. D. and REES, B. R. *Celtic Heritage*, London/New York, 1961.
RENFREW, C. *Before Civilisation. The radio-carbon revolution and prehistoric Europe*, London, 1973.
ROSS, A. *Pagan Celtic Britain*, London, 1974.
RHYS, Sir J. *Hibbert Lectures*, London, 1886.
—— *Celtic Folklore*, Oxford, 1901.
—— *Studies in the Arthurian Legend*, Oxford, 1891.
RICHEY, M. F. *Studies of Wolfram von Eschenbach*, London, 1957.
SJOESTEDT, M-L. (tr. M. Dillon) *Gods and Heroes of the Celts*, London, 1949.
SOMMER, H. O. (ed.) *The Vulgate Version of the Arthurian Romances* (7 vols.), Washington, D.C., 1909.
SQUIRE, C. *Celtic Myth and Legend. Poetry and Romance*, London, 1912.
STONE, J. F. S. *Wessex*, London, 1958.
THOM, A. *Megalithic Sites in Britain*, Oxford, 1967.
THOMAS, H. H. 'The Sources of the Stones of Stonehenge', *Antiquaries Journal* III (1923), 239–60.
THOMPSON, S. *The Folktale*, London/New York, 1946.
TOLKIEN, J. R. R. and GORDON, E. V. *Sir Gawaine and the Green Knight*, Oxford, 1930.
TURVILLE-PETRE, E. O. G. *Myth and Religion of the North*, London, 1964.
VERMASEREN, M. J. *Cybele and Attis. The Myth and the Cult*, London/New York, 1977.
VINAVER, E. *Malory*, Oxford, 1929.
WADE EVANS, A. W. *Emergence of England and Wales*, Cambridge, 1959.
WAINWRIGHT, F. T. (ed.) *The Problem of the Picts*, Edinburgh, 1955.
WATKINS, A. *The Old Straight Track*, London, 1976.
WESTON, J. L. *From Ritual to Romance*, Cambridge, 1920.
—— *The Quest of the Holy Grail*, London, 1913.
WILLIAMS, M. 'Apropos of an Episode in *Perlesvaus*', *Folk-Lore* 48 (London, 1937), 263–6.
WOOD, J. E. *Sun, Moon and Standing Stones*, Oxford/New York, 1978.
ZEYDEL, E. H. and MORGAN, B. O. *The Parzival of Wolfram von Eschenbach*, Chapel Hill, 1951.

Index

Abaris 83
abundance 49, 52, 56, 66, 67, 73, 74, 79
Adonis 41
adventure 48, 57, 58, 61, 62, 91, 117, 118, 123ff., 130, 131, 137
adventurous, bed 58; palace (Corbenic) 56; forest 127; locations 69
Alain 52, 56, 106
Alan, king of Brittany 54
Alaw 146
Alphisem, Alphisan see Galaphes
altars 15, 148
Ambr 87, 122
Ambrius, monastery of 112
Ambrosius, a title of Merlin 122, 123
Amesbury 16, 87, 122
Anfortas 55, 74, 75
Anglesey 146
Anglo-Saxon invasion 21, 142
Animals, lord of 29
Anna 129
anointing with blood 48, 49, 53, 98
Annwn (Annwm) 55, 78
antlers 15, 134
Apolin 99
Apollo 83, 84, 99
April 1st 119
Arawn 20
Arbroie 127
Arfon 20
Aries (cowherd), wife of 25
Arroy 127
Artemis 28
Arthur 7, 9, 10, 12, 13, 25, 38, 59, 87, 89, 90, 91
Arthur, historical 7, 9, 13, 21, 22, 105, 138; pre- or proto-historical 138
Arthurian cycle, legends, etc. 7, 8, 9, 14, 25, 26, 36, 38, 47, 51, 72, 74, 96, 97; origins of 74
Asia Minor 108, 109
Astarte 56
Astronomy 134, 136
August 28, 64
August 1st 98

Aurelius Ambrosius 16, 86, 87, 100, 111, 112
Avallach 79
Avallo, Avalloc 79
Avalon (Avaron) 52, 65, 77, 113
Avebury 17, 82
Avilion 65, 67; Vale of 12, 79, 126, 138
Avilion, Lady Lile of 68, 69
Axes 42, 57, 65, 69, 116; incised 93

Babylon 41, 47
Badon 12
Balan 34, 77, 90, 91, 116, 120, 121, 137
Balin 53, 75ff., 89ff., 116, 118ff.; 121, 137, 138; sword of 75, 91, 93, 94, 96, 98, 117, 139
Ban 39, 43, 44, 74, 75, 81, 115, 119, 120ff., 127, 133, 137
Barenton 76
barrenness 53ff., 66, 69, 70
Bath 134
Battle-Axe culture 93
Baudemagus 39, 74, 75, 120, 122
Beaker culture, beakers 93, 110, 141, 143
Beaumains 128
Bedegraine, Bedingran 22, 115
Beforet 38
beheading 42, 50, 54, 62, 67, 107
Belenton 76
Belenus 109, 118
Belgae 141, 142
Beli 57, 72, 73, 73, 75, 76, 91, 95, 100, 118, 119, 121, 122
Beli Mawr (Pellinore?) 75
Belias le Noir 35
Belinus 77
Beltain 118
Benwick 115, 120
Bilis 76
black 33, 35, 36; giant 29; hounds 124
Black Knight 30, 31, 33, 35, 69
blackthorn, knight of 68

blood 25, 47ff., 53, 69, 74, 76, 90, 91, 98, 111, 117, 132, 141
blood groups 110
Blue Knight 35
bluestone move 21, 24, 93, 106, 113, 141, 148
bluestones 16, 55, 87, 94, 95, 96, 133, 138, 139
boar's tooth helmet 24
boat, Pellinore wounded in 55
boat burial 132, 138, 139
Boia 15, 127
Bolgios 77, 109
Boreadae 83, 123
Boreas 83, 122, 123
Bors, Bohors, etc. (King) 115, 121ff., 133, 137
Bors, Bohort, etc. (Sir) 44, 57, 61, 63, 64, 68, 75, 121, 123, 128, 129
bough, broken 27, 67
brachet 124
Bragwaine 128
Bramans (i.e. Brahmins) 37
Bran 15, 39, 51, 64, 72ff., 77, 81, 100, 107, 113, 114, 119ff., 125, 127, 129, 130, 146
Bran de Lis 74
branch, see bough
Brandegoris 115, 119, 120
Brandel 120
Brandigan 74
Brandiles 120, 129; sister of 137
Brandus des Illes 74
Brangemeur 74
Brangoire 63, 64, 75, 113, 123, 133; daughter of 63, 64, 128, 137
Brangor 74
Branwen 87, 128, 146ff.
Brennius 74, 77
Brennos 77, 109
Breton storytellers 14
bridges 35, 61
Brien 74
Britons 9, 12, 14, 16, 86, 142
Brittany 14, 76, 77, 84, 132, 134
Broceliande 76
Bron 52, 74, 106, 107
Bronze Age 24, 82, 88, 139,

140, 142; Early 17, 85, 95, 138, 143, 144; Wessex 18, literature 9, 18, 88
bull-horned gods 15
burning, death by 40, 41, 50, 141
Burning City 40, 41, 45, 46, 51, 68, 70

Cadbury Castle 13, 21, 22, 96
Caladbolg (Caledvwlch) 116, 118
Caliburn, Caliburnus 116
Cambenet, Duke of 115
Cameliard (Carmelide) 124
Camelot 7ff., 12ff., 21, 22, 106, 116, 117, 124, 126, 130, 131, 134, 135, 139, 140
Camlan 12, 77
Candlemas 115, 119
cannibalism 50, 147, 148
Carados, King of 115
Carawent en Gales 61
Carbonek, see Corbenic
Cardot, Carduel, etc. 22, 112, 125, 134
Carmarthen 111
Caroaise 124
cart 58ff., 64, 69, 70, 81, 123, 129
Castle of the Border 22
Castle Perilous 129, 131
Castle of the White Thorn 22
castration 54ff., 66, 75
cauldron of inspiration 78; of regeneration 73
Cavallon, the king's sister 65
Celtic culture 109, 111; speech 111; traditional tales 8, 9, 15, 62, 104
Celts 140
ceremonial 37, 41, 42, 47, 50, 90, 105, 106, 129
challenge knight 87, 129, 131, 132
challenge theme 10, 24–36 passim, 37, 39, 45, 46, 53, 65, 67, 68, 76, 91, 117, 124, 128, 130, 131
charette (chariot) 58, 60, 61
childlessness 55
children of Don 126
Chrétien de Troyes 10, 11, 28, 55, 58ff., 66, 148
Christ 44, 46, 50, 51
Christmas 112
clearing in forest, see glade
Colombe 90
conception 62ff., 66, 78, 79, 112, 113, 129
Conchobar 113
copulation 62, 64, 78, 79, 113
Corbenic (Carbonek) 22, 48,

49, 52, 56, 57, 63, 65, 92, 98, 107, 120
Cordelia 73, 80
Cornwall, the Cornish 14, 81, 112, 115, 128, 145
Cradelmas 115
Creiddylad 73
criminals 61
cromlech 140
crow 78
cults, native (see also sacred waters, head cult and challenge theme) 8, 72, 79
cult sites (see also ford, fountain, etc.) 15, 25, 33, 35, 76, 129
cup, bowl, etc. 30, 46, 49, 50
custom of castle, the 25, 49, 90
cymbal 35, 67, 68
Cynon 29

Dame of the Lake 81
Damsel of the Lake 79, 81
Danann 95, 109
dance (see also Giants' Dance) 64, 83, 85, 90
Danu 95
Danube 109
Dark Ages 7, 17ff., 25, 97, 99, 125
David, St 15
death 15, 61, 62
deities (see also gods and goddesses) 9, 19, 22, 60, 62, 64, 65, 69, 72–81 passim, 85, 107, 119, 121, 133, 137ff.
Delians 83
Denmark (Danemarche) 124
deposition of treasure in water 109
Diana 7, 26, 27, 28, 79, 80, 134
Diane 79, 134
Dianus (Janus) 79, 80
Diarwya 127
Diodorus Siculus 83, 84, 122
Dione 80, 134
dismemberment 62
Do, Dos, Doon 125
Dodone 38
dog 126
Dolorous Stroke, the 7, 9, 53–71 passim, 76, 90, 91, 107, 117
Dolorous Tower, the 22
Don (goddess) 19, 72, 95, 109, 111, 125, 126, 130, 134
Don (river) 95, 109, 111
Drunemeton 109
dwarf 40
Dyfed 20, 55, 76, 134
Dyonas 79, 80

earth mother 93
Easter 115, 119

eaten god, cult of 51
Egeria 28, 79
Elaine 64, 81, 128
Elaine, Bran's wife 43, 81, 121
Elaine, the Damsel of the Lake 79, 81
Elaine, Igraine's daughter 81, 113, 114, 137
Elaine, Pelles's daughter 43, 63, 81, 107, 128, 137
Eleine, daughter of Pellinore and the Lady of the Rule 25, 81
Elene 128
emasculation 55, 123
Emrys 122
enchantment 12, 52, 77
England, English 14, 126, 132
Epona 55
equinoxes 98, 119; vernal 83
Esclados le Ros 34
Estorause 44
Euangelische Eucharist 50, 52, 69
Evaine 121
Evelake 106, 107
Evrain 74
Excalibur 115ff., 139

Far Away Isles, King of 68
fays 77, 78
feast/festival 37, 56, 64, 91, 98, 113, 118, 124, 125, 126, 131, 132; of Diana 28
February 1st 98, 119
fecundity 15, 64, 66
fertility 28, 63, 77
fiery man 56, 57, 92, 107, 118
filth 61, 64, 69, 123, 129
fir tree 35
fish, meal of 51, 106, 108, 141
Fisher King (see also Rich Fisher) 48, 51, 52, 54ff., 64, 66, 73ff., 98, 107, 122, 144
flaming weapon 57ff., 61, 69, 116, 118, 129
floated stones 13, 117, 131, 139, 148
fogou (souterrain) 145
folklore 38; folk memory 16; folk-tales 15, 38, 76
footholder 19ff.
fords 15, 20, 21, 26, 35ff., 55, 59, 67ff., 78, 79, 137
foreknowledge 12
forest clearing, see glade
fountains 26, 29ff., 35, 45, 68ff., 76, 79, 92, 93, 123, 127, 129, 130, 137
Fountain Stone 43
fourteen year period 68
France 10, 14, 109
Frazer, Sir J. 7, 19, 26, 35, 37, 40, 79, 102, 139

French medieval poets 13, 14, 21, 22, 38, 97, 116
French traditional tales (*see also* 'matter of Britain') 8, 9, 21, 36, 79
fruitfulness 37

Gaheris 130
Galabes, fountain of 86
Galahad, King (Launcelot's grandfather) 44, 45, 108
Galahad (Sir) 43ff., 53, 57, 62, 64, 68, 70, 81, 91, 98, 101, 107, 108, 113, 117, 118, 121, 123, 126, 131
Galaphes / Alphisan / Kalafes 52, 56, 57, 92, 93, 106, 107, 117, 118, 122, 124
Galatia 108, 109, 111
Gales 108, 110
Galicia 108, 109, 111
Galli 108, 140
Gannes 121
Gareth 65, 129, 137
garland 67
Gaul, Gauls 83, 108, 109, 110, 115, 121, 142
Gawaine 34, 57, 58, 61, 65, 68, 69, 91, 108, 124, 126, 129, 137
Gawaine and the Green Knight 77
Geoffrey of Monmouth 10, 16ff., 73, 77, 80, 85ff., 89, 100, 101, 105, 122, 129, 148
Germany 60
Gewissae 86
Giants 17, 74, 86, 146; black 29
Giants' Dance 16, 18, 23, 24, 86, 87, 89, 92ff., 100, 101, 105, 112, 120, 122, 133
Giflet (Griflet le Fise de Dieu) 125
gifts 83, 85
Gilfaethwy son of Don 19, 20, 126
Gilloman 86, 87
Giraldus Cambresis 77
glades 15, 26, 29, 30, 34, 35, 65, 67, 68, 79, 81, 125, 129, 131
Glastonbury 52; Tor 81
goat-horned gods 15
goddesses 15, 55, 56, 60, 65, 72–81 *passim*, 113, 120, 126ff., 132, 134, 138, 144
gods 15, 39, 53, 57, 58, 62, 65, 72–81 *passim*, 113, 114, 118, 121ff., 138, 144
gold 42, 44, 63, 70, 127
Golden Bough, The 26
good luck 15
Gore 113, 115, 119, 120
Grail, sangreal, etc. 44ff., 53,

56, 63, 69, 70, 94, 106, 112, 113, 118
grail-bearer 47, 48, 58, 62
Grail Castle 48, 56, 57, 61, 67, 69, 75, 117, 118, 129, 134
grail hero 93, 94
grail keepers 48, 52, 56, 57, 75, 107
Grail King 74
grail procession 50, 56, 98, 106, 107
Grail Quest 9, 48, 53, 64, 70, 75, 91, 97, 117
grail seekers 48, 52, 57, 62, 64ff., 75, 123
grail table 57, 70
Grassholm 78
graves 90, 130, 146
Greece, Greeks 16, 62, 72, 83, 84, 109, 123, 140
green 36, 59; knight 35, 69
grey 35, 36
groves 15, 26, 27, 60, 61, 79, 83, 85, 109, 134
Guenever, Guinivere 38, 58, 59, 120, 121, 124, 130, 132
Guiglain 129
Gurguran 50, 147, 148
Gwales 120
Gwern 147
Gwydion, Son of Don 19, 20
Gwyn 73
Gwynedd 19
gysarm 65, 129

Hades 119
Hafgan 35
hagiography 127
hags 9, 78, 127
Hallowe'en 41, 63
Hallstatt culture 141, 142
hammer 57, 116
hart, white 124, 129
head, severed, cult of 14, 39, 46, 75, 81, 120
heads in wells 21, 36, 39, 45, 46, 67, 68, 130; on stakes 67
healing, health 15, 77, 79, 86, 98
Hecateus 83, 84, 122, 123
heelstone 98
Helain le Blanc 63, 64, 113, 121
Helen 81, 140
Helena 81
Helie 128
henges 95
Henry of Huntingdon 16
heroes 61, 62, 65, 66, 72, 79, 102, 105, 112, 113, 120, 121, 123, 129, 133, 138, 140
heroines 52, 102, 105, 129, 140
hero-tales 62

Hibernia 120
hill-forts 95
Hocelice (Hosseliche) 108, 110
Homer 9, 17, 24, 140
Hontzlake 126
Hood, Robin 12
horned gods 15
horns blown 35, 65, 67, 68, 90, 124, 129, 131
Hyperboreans 83, 84

Iblis 38
idolatry 97
Igerne, Igraine 112, 113, 137
immigration 110
impotency 55
India 37, 95
Indo-European influence, origin of 24, 80, 82, 93, 95, 111, 118, 132, 139, 144; languages 95
Ireland, Irish 16, 62, 72, 73, 84, 86, 87, 92, 93, 95, 108, 120, 134, 146
Ireland, King of 87, 94, 120, 124, 128, 129, 135, 139, 147; King's son of 92, 94, 117, 128; Queen of 87
Irish literature 57, 62, 72, 73, 78
Iron Age 22, 95, 109ff., 142; Early 85
Iseult (Queen of Ireland's daughter) 137, 145
Islands 34ff., 60, 61, 67, 68, 74, 76, 78, 79, 81, 91, 117, 124, 128, 129; Faraway Isles 68
Ivernia 120
Iweret 34, 38

Jana 80
Janus 79, 80
Joseph of Arimathea 44, 46, 48, 51, 52, 56, 101, 106ff., 112, 120, 141ff.
Josephe 106, 112, 117, 118
joy 39, 40, 42, 65, 70, 87, 90
jubilee 37
Juno 80
Jupiter 79, 80, 99
jusarm 65

Kalafes, *see* Galaphes
Kay 130
Keltoi 108
Killare 16, 86, 87
kings, kingship annual, *see under* annual; sacred, divine – *see under* sacred; priestly 7
king of the wood 26, 28, 35, 79

La Tène culture 141

Labor, Lambor 54, 107, 122
Lady of the Castle Perilous 137
Lady of the Fountain 31, 32, 68, 137
Lady of the Fountain, The 11 28ff., 68, 128, 131
Lady of the Lake 43, 63, 64, 68, 81, 89, 123, 126, 138
Lady of the Rule 25, 81, 129
Lady of Shalott 138
lake 12, 68
Lambor see Labor
Lamorak 130
Lanceor 89, 90
Latona 83, 85
Launcelot (Sir) 9, 38ff., 54, 57ff., 62, 64, 68, 75, 81, 122, 128, 129, 131, 137
Launcelot (King), Sir Launcelot's grandfather 43
Lear 73, 80
legends, see under Arthurian, Welsh, etc.
lenition 120
Leodegrance, Leodegan 120, 124
lightning 57, 73, 76, 80, 93, 116, 118, 134; cult 93; god 69, 80, 93, 118, 132; spear 76, 123; sword 76, 117; symbol 93, 94, 138
lime tree 35, 38
Linet 128, 131
lion 29
Lioness 65, 129, 131
literature, Bronze Age 9, 17, 95
literature, oral 8, 13, 20, 88, 140
Lleu 72
Lludd 73, 114, 119
Llyr 73
Logris, Logres 54, 70, 97, 134
London 21, 115
long life 73
Lot 114, 115, 119, 124, 127, 130, 133, 137
Lothian 115
love-making 65, 66
Luned 32, 128, 131

Mabinogion, The 8, 11, 18, 19, 36, 69, 72, 74, 76, 127, 146
Mabon 72, 78, 84, 85, 99
Mabonagrain 85
Macedonia 77, 109
magic (see also enchantment) 46, 52, 53, 54, 56, 64, 66, 70, 85
Mahommed, Mahoumerie, etc. 99, 100
Maimed King 48, 49, 51, 52,

53–71 passim, 75, 81, 91, 98, 107, 117, 122, 132, 134
Malory, Sir Thomas 8ff., 14, 21, 38, 43, 45, 50, 55, 58, 63, 66, 106, 112, 116, 119ff., 124, 129, 140
Malgiers li Gris 34
Man, Isle of 74
Maponius 84
Marche, Castle of 63ff., 67, 68, 70
Marhalt 128
Marhaus 126, 128, 129
Marigart le Rous 34
Mark 90, 128, 145
Mars 82
Math 19, 20
'matter of Britain' (Matière de Bretagne) 9, 10, 14ff., 18ff., 36, 38, 39, 43, 46, 47, 54, 55, 61, 62, 65, 66, etc.
Maugys 34
May 1st, Maying 58, 59, 73, 98, 101, 112, 118, 119
meal, ritual 48, 106
megalithic construction 134; period 84, 96, 98, 99, 131
Mela, Pomponius 77
Meleagant 59, 122; sister of 39, 75
Meliagrance 59, 130
Merchant's Table 135
Merlin 12, 16, 25, 80, 86, 87, 89ff., 111ff., 133–36 passim, 137, 138
metamorphosis 77ff.
Middle Ages 18, 77, 86, 100
midnight 63
midsummer 98
Miles of the Glade 125
minstrels, minstrelsy 61, 70, 90
Modron 72, 78, 79, 85
Mont St Michel 76, 81
moon 83, 84, 128
Mordred 9, 12, 113, 129
Morgan le Fay 77ff., 113, 120, 127
Morgawse 113, 129
Morgne the goddess 77
Morrigan 78
Morte Darthur 10, 11, 13, 38, 53, 58, 91, 116, 119
Mother Earth 60
mother goddess 78, 82, 144
mound 29, 69
music 20, 37, 39, 41, 70, 83, 85
Mycenae, Mycenaean 17, 18, 24, 82, 140
Myrddin 122
myth, mythology 8, 18, 19, 25, 38, 47, 62, 73, 74, 105, 117, 119, 121, 138, 141

Nemeton place names 109
Nemetona 80
Nemi 7, 26ff., 35, 36, 67, 79
Neolithic Age 82, 110, 142, 144
Neolithic causewayed enclosures 95
Nerthus (Mother Earth) 60, 61
New year's day 39, 40, 98, 115, 119
Nimue 79, 126
nine priestesses 77, 78
noon 42
north wind 123
Northumberland 89, 115, 131
November 1st 98
nymph 28, 79ff., 134

oak-god, -goddess 79
offal 21, 123, 129
Ogyrvran 120
one-eyed, one-legged 29
Ontzlake 126
oracle 77
oral tales, tradition, etc. 8, 10, 13, 15, 18, 24, 41, 61, 67, 70, 76, 85, 87, 96, 104
Orkney 114, 115
otherworld 9, 19, 20, 55, 79
Owein 30ff., 69, 78, 85, 120, 122, 127, 128, 137

pagan dogma 51
pagan king crowned 22
Palamides 120
Pantheon 138, 144; Roman 82
Parzival 55
Pedryvan 120
Pellam 53, 90
Pelleas 129
Pellehan 107
Pelles 44, 48, 55, 63ff., 75, 76, 81, 87, 98, 107, 133
Pellinore 12, 25, 55, 75, 76, 81, 122, 124ff., 129, 130, 133, 136, 137
Pembrokeshire 85, 87, 92
Pentecost (see Whitsuntide)
Perceval 10
Percival 44, 57, 68, 122, 129, 137
Percival le Gallois 55
Percival's father 55; sister 49, 50, 91, 138
Perilous locations, see adventurous
Perlesvaus 50
peron 89, 90, 91, 94, 96, 99, 100, 117, 130, 139
Pescheour, Petchere 66, 98
Pictish language 110

pigs, obtained by deception 19
pine tree 35, 67, 100
planets 136
plenty, *see* abundance
post-Roman era 7, 13, 16, 21, 25, 38, 100, 130, 138, 141
Prescelly Mountains 17, 55, 85, 87, 120
priesthood, priestess, etc. 17, 26, 27, 129
procession 20, 42, 49, 70, 105
prosperity 15, 53, 55, 64, 66
Proud One of the Clearing 68
Pryderi 19
Pwyll 20, 35ff., 55, 76, 127

Questing Beast 25, 130
Quilacare 37, 40, 41

rainmaking charm 29, 33
red 35, 36, 42, 70, 91, 98, 117, 118; City 22; Knight 35, 65, 70, 129, 131; Laund 65
Rhiannon 55
Rich Fisher (*see also* Fisher King) 51, 52, 66, 70, 107, 144
Rience, Ryons, etc. 89, 90, 116, 120, 124, 139
Rig Veda 95
ritual acts 67, 75, 139; cannibalism 50, 147, 148; castration 56; combat 26; copulation 62, 113; death 48, 105, 132, 147; meals 48, 51, 70, 141; vehicles 60, 61, 69; vessels 50, 58, 69, 132
river crossing (*see also* bridge, ford) 34, 124
Robert de Boron 10
Robin Hood 12
roebuck 126
Roevent en Gales 64
Roman Britain, Roman occupation 7, 14, 15, 17, 82, 85, 110, 141, 143
romance, romances 7, 9, 10–21, 58, 74, 75, 89, 104, 119, 127
Rome, Romans 72, 79, 109
Round Table 9, 112, 113, 116, 120, 124–33, 135, 136, 137, 139, 143, 148
Rule, the Lady of 24, 25, 81, 129

Sabrina 120
sacred kings, kingship 19, 20, 37, 41, 45, 53ff., 67ff., 75, 91, 98, 100, 104, 118, 122, 130, 134
sacred waters, cult of 15, 39,
92, 109, 137
sacred waters, cult of 15, 39, 92, 109, 137
sacrifice 37, 53, 56, 61, 69
Saint Carannog 148; David 15; 127: David's 87; Michael's Mount 81; Stephen's church 98, 116, 124, 141; feast 98
Salisbury 21, 112; Plain 85, 99, 100, 112, 116, 131ff., 137, 138, 140, 141
Samhuin 98
'Saracen' 54, 115, 130
Sarras, Sarrasens 22, 44, 49, 68, 89–103 *passim*, 106, 117, 121, 123, 143
Sarsen 17, 100, 139, 140
Savage Mountain 68
Saxons 9, 12, 16, 86, 101, 102, 111, 112, 115
scabbard, magic 12, 89, 107
Scotland, King of 115
scourge 61, 129
sea transport of bluestones 87
Sein (Sena) 77, 78
serpent 29, 58
Sesnes 101
seven year period 37, 68, 128, 129
severed heads 14, 15, 39, 42, 45, 46, 73, 74, 81, 125
Severn, river 120, 148
sexuality 65
shapeshifting 12, 13
ship 107, 126
shoes, old 61, 64, 123, 129
Siege Perilous (*see under* perilous)
silver 70
Skellig Michael 81
skull, human, in cult well 15
sky-god 93
social organization 95
solstice 98, 99, 119
song, singing 20, 58, 83, 85
Sorhaute 115
sorrow 41, 42
Spain 108, 109
spear 45, 47ff., 53, 57, 98, 107, 116
Spring (the season) 36, 118, 132
springs 15, 26, 38, 67, 134
stag 29
stag-headed/horned 115, 122
stars 136
stone circles 17
Stonehenge 16, 17, 55, 82, 84, 92ff., 96, 98ff., 122, 123, 136, 139, 143
stones 15, 57; floated or erected 13, 89ff., 99

storm god 58
Stranggore 115, 119
suitor 38
Summer 35, 36
sun 84, 129; -temple 98
supernatural 12, 77, 78, 128, 132
superstition 85
sword 51, 54, 75, 89, 107, 116; Balin's, *see* Balin; drawn from stone 7, 9, 91ff., 97, 115–23 *passim*, 126, 137; taken from lake 12; thrown into lake 137
sycamore 35, 65, 67, 129, 131
Syria 41, 56

taboos 55
Tacitus 60
Taliesin 120
Tammuz 41
Taranis 99
temples 37, 41, 60, 68, 83, 98, 123; sun-oriented 93
Tennyson 9, 14, 40
Terice 100
Terre Foraine 52, 56, 62, 106, 107, 117
Terre Gaste, *see* Waste Land
Tervagant 99, 100
thighs, wound in 51, 55, 56, 63, 65, 67, 73, 75, 87, 107, 126, 129
Thor 57, 116
thorn tree 35, 67
three-faced head 80
thunder, thunderbolt 30, 57, 58, 80, 98, 116, 118, 122
thunder-god 93
Tintagel 112
Toledo, council of 15
tomb 35, 68; entrance 69
Tombelaine 76
Tor 25, 124
tradition (*see also* Welsh, Arthurian, oral, etc.) 13, 14, 25, 50, 51, 79, 96, 107
tournaments 63, 64, 75, 137
Trebes 22
tree, single, significant 15, 26, 27, 30, 33, 38, 67, 68, 104, 146
triple form 78
Tristan 10
Tristan 148
Tristram 105, 128, 129, 145
Tristramssaga 145
Twelfth Night 115
Two-faced heads 80

Uriens, Ryons, etc. 113, 115, 120, 122, 127, 130, 137

Urnfield culture 141
Uther Ben 120
Uther Pendragon 16, 18, 87, 111, 112, 115, 120, 124, 125, 131, 133
Uwaine 127, 130

Vandeberes 22
vehicles, ritual 60, 61, 69
vessels, ritual 50, 58, 69, 132
virginity 7, 20, 28, 44, 49, 64, 66, 67, 77, 127
virility 66ff.
Vivienne 79
Vortigern 80, 86, 111, 112; his son 87

Wales 14, 19, 21, 62, 78, 92, 95, 108, 111, 112, 126, 135, 147; North 19, 115, 116, 124, 131; South-west 16, 76, 85, 87, 134; Welsh people 110

war 15
warrior gods 82
washer at ford 78
waste city 41, 42, 45, 46, 54, 66, 68, 70
Waste Land 35, 54, 56, 57, 66, 107, 108, 122, 138
water (see also ford, fountain, island, lake, river, well) 35, 68, 70, 74, 79; water-fay 38
weather control 77, 79
wells 15, 25, 35, 39, 45, 67, 75, 81, 104, 126, 130, 146; well cult 46, 70; well-maidens 70
well-being 37, 72
Welsh tradition and traditional tales 8, 9, 14, 18ff., 38, 54, 55, 62, 72ff., 76, 78, 95, 113, 126, 129, 130, 132
Wessex 18, 143; culture 139, 141, 143
white 35, 36, 70, dove 57;

hart 124, 126; knight 70; palfrey 124, 126; phantom 132
Whitsuntide 87, 91, 112, 115, 117ff., 126, 131
Wiltshire 100
Winchester 21
winter 36; solstice 98, 99
witches 9
wizards, wizardry 17, 111

year, Celtic 98; death and rebirth of 82
year-end battle 20, 21, 36, 37, 55; beheading 54; bonfires 41; death 37–52 passim, 91
Ynys Veli 73
Yvain 10, 11, 28

Zeus 57, 80, 116, 122; a more barbaric 93; native 98, 117, 122

DATE DUE			
MAR 1 9 1990			
JUN 3 0 1992			
OCT 1 2 1993			

AUG - 7 1995

GAYLORD FR2